The Open University

A220 Princes and Peoples: France and the British Isles, 1620–1714

Block 1: Traditional society and the civil wars, 1620s–1640s

First published in 1994 by
The Open University
Walton Hall
Milton Keynes
United Kingdom
MK7 6AA

© 1994 The Open University

Reprinted 1999, 2000, 2002

ISBN 0 7492 8548 6

Edited, designed and typeset by The Open University.

This book is a component of the Open University course A220 *Princes and Peoples: France and the British Isles, 1620–1714*. Details of this and other Open University courses are available from the Central Enquiry Service, The Open University, PO Box 200, Walton Hall, MK7 6YZ, tel.: 0908 653078.

Printed and bound in the United Kingdom by the Alden Group, Oxford

A220/B1/2.3

28109C/a220blpli2.3

Contents

SCOTLAND

Forth
Edinburgh
Glasgow
Clyde

Carrickfergus

ULSTER

CONNAUGHT

Galway
Shannon
Liffey
Dublin

LEINSTER

MUNSTER

Cork

E N G L A N D

York

Chester

W A L E S
Severn

Norwich

Cardiff

Bristol

London
Thames

0   50   100   150 kms
0   50   100 miles

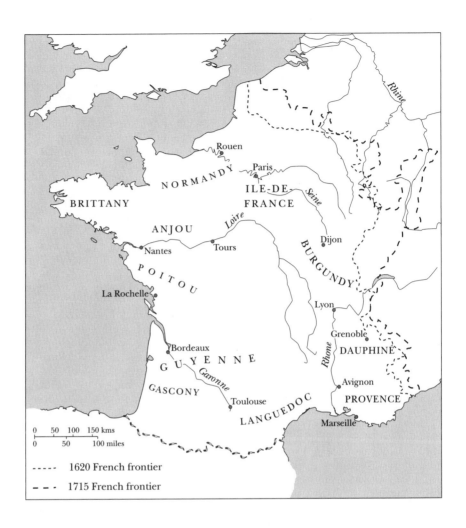

ROUEN

Paris

NORMANDY

ILE-DE-
FRANCE

Seine

BRITTANY

ANJOU

Loire

Dijon

Nantes

Tours

BURGUNDY

POITOU

La Rochelle

Lyon

Rhône

Grenoble

DAUPHINE

Bordeaux

GUYENNE

Garonne

Avignon

GASCONY

Toulouse

PROVENCE

LANGUEDOC

Marseille

Rhône

| 0 | 50 | 100 | 150 kms |
| 0 | 50 | | 100 miles |

- - - - - 1620 French frontier

- - - 1715 French frontier

General introduction

The aim of the course is to study France and the British Isles in the period 1620–1714 with a view to understanding what kinds of state each had become by the later seventeenth century. I don't think that we are begging the question by saying that, despite great similarities, there were also very marked differences, yet both states went on, in the eighteenth century, to become world powers. France is characterized in 1714 as an absolutist state, while Britain is characterized as a limited monarchy. In this course we shall investigate what these terms mean and whether these are satisfactory descriptions of the two states in 1714. So our course aims are to consider:

1   what kinds of state emerged in France and the British Isles in the period 1620–1714;

2   how these states developed.

This, the first of the three blocks of the course, is devoted to the civil wars of the mid-seventeenth century in France and the British Isles. We shall concentrate on the events of the early seventeenth century, how they unfolded into war, and on the short-term consequences of the wars. In the second block we shall look at the mentalities and at the local communities of the societies of seventeenth-century France and the British Isles; in the third block we shall look at the processes by which France and the British Isles developed into different kinds of state. Throughout the course we shall be looking at the sources which historians use to try to understand the developments of the past. In the units and the audiocassettes we shall concentrate upon written sources. In the TV and video we shall concentrate upon buildings and artefacts of the period.

The course components

The three blocks of the course (Units 1–16), are your guide to studying the histories of France and the British Isles in the period 1620–1714. Much of the historical background to the specific topics discussed in the units is provided in two of the set books: Coward, *The Stuart Age*, and Briggs, *Early Modern France 1560–1715* (henceforth referred to as Coward and Briggs respectively). These are recent text books by respected historians in their fields and we shall also be using them to consider different historical interpretations. You will be directed to read sections from them at different points of the course. Since they do not cover Scotland, Ireland and Wales, you may expect to find more information about these countries given in the course units. But these books are not simply there to give you information, they are also intended to show you how historians approach their subject and work out their explanations for historical developments. You will find the work of other historians supplied in the offprints of articles which accompany the course material.

Historians require original documents and other materials dating from the period they are studying. We are providing you with a variety of different kinds of primary source. First, there is the third set book, the *Anthology* of documents. The documents are all from the period under investigation, but will seem rather different because the English documents appear as they were originally (with the spelling and capitalization standardized), and the Scottish documents appear with some adjustments whilst the French documents have been translated into modern English. Some of the audio-cassettes will be used to study particular documents in detail. We are also giving you some seventeenth-century debates on audio-cassette.

We are placing a great emphasis upon visual sources: the evidence of the material world of the seventeenth century. Such sources (buildings, sculpture, paintings, household goods, and landscape) have long been studied by art historians, archaeologists, and historical geographers. It is only fairly recently that they have been much exploited by social and economic historians. We are presenting you, in the videos and the TV programmes, with a variety of different kinds of visual source, sources which increasingly social historians use as evidence of the material circumstances of people's lives. For example, portraits might tell you something about the appearance of the sitter, about fashions in clothing and about techniques of painting and changes in artistic style. What they will certainly tell you, however, is a great deal about the aspirations of the person who commissioned the painting. Likewise, buildings can tell you much about the aspirations of the builder and of later occupants, even at a comparatively lowly level. But it is necessary to learn to 'read' such sources because the information they contain requires decoding.

At the beginning of each unit you will be told what components of the course you will need for that particular unit. The exception to this is the TV programmes. These have been sent to you on cassette so you may more conveniently view them, but they will probably be broadcast during the year as well. You should watch these programmes over the first eight weeks of the course. As you work through the video exercises in association with the units you will find that topics discussed in the TV programmes will be developed in more detail. You will find that returning to the TV programmes at the end of the course will help you to revise and to bring together the general themes of the course.

Unit 1
Society and government on the eve of the civil wars

Prepared for the course team by
Anne Laurence

Contents

Study timetable

Weeks of study	Texts	Video	AC	Set books
2	Unit 1, *Anthology* I.1,2,3,4, Offprint 1, Illustration Book	Video 1	AC1, section 1	Coward, Briggs

During the period of this unit you should also watch TV1 and 2.

The objectives of this unit are that you should:

1   understand something of how historians study the seventeenth century and the kinds of evidence they use;

2   understand what is involved in *your* study of seventeenth-century France and the British Isles;

3   understand some definitions of key terms in the course;

4   understand something of the nature of the early seventeenth-century state and its institutions and the extent of the state's power in France and the British Isles.

Introduction to historical study

The task of the historian

Historians are not simply engaged in the process of reconstructing, minute by minute, the passage of the past. They are engaged in trying to analyse what happened, and to explain how it came about. Historians discover new material and think in new ways about such traditional concerns as the politics or religion of the past. But they also enlarge historical knowledge by asking new questions of the past, questions sometimes influenced by our contemporary concerns as citizens, with old age or gender issues, for example.

Historians constantly seek to demonstrate the validity of their analysis by close reference to the materials of the past. Their work is part of an overall contribution to a body of knowledge about the past in general and about specific periods, subjects and debates in particular. They use their specialized knowledge of sources to respond to the work of other historians and to advance everyone's understanding of the past.

Arthur Marwick (1990, p.242) has described historians' writing as involving narrative, analysis and description and has stressed the difficulty of achieving a satisfactory balance between them. Narrative is the re-telling of a sequence of events or the stages of a process, but merely listing *what* happened does not explain *why* it happened. Much thought and effort goes into ascribing causes to complex developments in the past and it is this that constitutes the analysis.

The balance between narrative and analysis is a difficult one to set because the two are often done simultaneously. The need to make this remark highlights something which distinguishes history from some of the other arts disciplines which you may have studied already. Historians do not have a ready defined subject in the sense of an *oeuvre*, the accumulation of the works of a writer or painter. In a loose way historians define their subjects according to certain conventions regarding historical periods, but these conventions are different for different types of history: social and economic historians, concerned with fundamental changes to society and the economy which took place over decades and sometimes centuries, use very different time-spans from historians of politics. Historians working on the history of women are increasingly finding that the conventional divisions of the past used for the history of male institutions and cultural developments have little relevance to women. The author of the article entitled 'Did women have a Renaissance?' (Kelly, 1984) was not asking a facetious question. Defining the subject is an important part of the historian's task.

Historians use description in connection with the sources or methods of analysis that they are using. For example, historians often derive data from sources which were originally intended to yield some completely different kind of information. In such cases it is generally necessary to describe the source in some detail. For example, receipts for the payment of arrears to soldiers who had served in the parliamentary armies during the English civil war give information about the length of soldiers' service and the organization of the armies, but they have also been used for trying to gather some idea of the level of literacy because the soldiers had to sign a receipt. There are other forms of description, too. This unit contains a certain amount of description of institutions in early modern France and the British Isles, as well as definitions of terms we shall be using in the course.

The historians whose writing you will read in the units, in the set books (Briggs and Coward), and in the offprints collection are all working within these conventions. But is this the same as what you will be doing? Up to a point, yes. If you did the Arts Foundation course you will find that some of the work in this course is similar, but done in a more specialized context. You will be reading, making notes, and trying to organize your ideas to answer the questions set in the exercises and assignments. Just as historians who work through boxes of documents are selective, so we expect you to be selective. We shall be asking you to consider specific problems, expressed in the exercises in the units, the audio-cassettes and video-tapes, and in the TMAs. You will need to have read, listened to, or watched, specified parts of the course and will then have to choose what is relevant to the problem in hand.

You will be asked to analyse historical developments, not to write narrative or description. You will never be asked to write down everything you know about a subject. If you are asked to compare Richelieu's domestic reforms with those of Thomas Wentworth you will not need to give a detailed description of what those reforms were, you need merely to refer to them in your analysis. You will not need to write about other aspects of their policies or to give their life histories. You will always be asked to address a specific problem or issue, so select what you want to say about it.

Comparative history

Our concern in this course is to look at two states, to compare and contrast them, and also to look at the kinds of changes which took place over the period 1620–1714. Neither France nor the British Isles was a single, homogeneous society and we shall be looking at the regional and national differences within the states. In particular, we shall be exploring questions about the development of the state. The course team believes that by comparing developments in more than one country we can illuminate issues more than if we were simply to confine ourselves to a single country. We believe that comparison will help you:

*   to learn more about underlying similarities and differences between the political, economic, and social structures of the countries;

*   to explore the common characteristics of political events such as the civil wars of England, Wales, Scotland, and Ireland and the Frondes in France;

*   to explore the common characteristics of such longer-term developments as concern for public order and the extension of the power of the state, in order to try to understand early modern mentalities;

*   to tackle the kinds of question which only make sense in a comparative context, such as why the French monarchy became absolutist whilst Britain developed a limited monarchy, while both developed into great powers.

We shall deal with complex developments in societies which are at once familiar because they produced the culture in which we live, and very distant because of the different material and ideological circumstances in which people lived then. Inevitably, given the time-span and the geographical scope of the course, we have had to leave things out. By confining ourselves to questions concerned with the development of the state we have not done justice to such subjects as the history of women or of religious dissidence. We have also only a limited amount of material on relations *between* the British Isles and France.

There is a great difference in the kinds of history written in the two countries. Crudely, this difference was characterized by Yves-Marie Bercé, 'Not so long ago, when the history of the seventeenth century was still taught … ' (Bercé, 1990, p.1). This somewhat opaque remark refers to the fact that in France there has been an increasing tendency, partly inspired by the work of the historians who established the influential journal, *Annales: économies, societés, civilizations,* for historians in France to concentrate upon long-term developments leading to social and economic change rather than on shorter-term political developments. Much of the recent work on political institutions in France has been done by historians in the English-speaking world. This difference in historical approaches means that often there is no directly comparable work on the institutions of the various countries. Because this course has been devised by historians working in Britain, our questions are often asked from the point of view of British concerns rather than French concerns, though in our consideration of social and economic structures in Block 2 we are reflecting the influence of French historians.

Comparison is an essential tool for historians. You will notice that, throughout your reading, historians make comparisons between places and across times. For example, Briggs on pp.10–11 contrasts the development of England with that of France and on p.11 compares the development of Protestantism in the two countries. Now turn to Coward and read pp.43–66.

Exercise   What kinds of comparison does Coward make in this passage?

Discussion   Coward compares the different social orders with each other (peers and gentry on pp.44–5, for example). He makes contrasts over time (on pp.45–6, for example, he draws attention to a change in the role of lesser gentlemen in the unusual circumstances of 1640). He writes about a historical debate (p.46) in which some historians argued that the wealth of great landowners was declining whilst others argued that these landowners were prospering. He makes comparisons between places, for example in discussing landowners in London and in the country (p.46), and between townspeople and country people (pp.58–9), and different regions of England (p.63).

Notice that Coward uses comparison to comment upon similarities as well as differences. He makes many different kinds of comparison, so you may see that it is impossible to deal with historical change without making comparisons. Look at the figures from Thomas Wilson on p.44. We can see how large the different social groups were relative to each other in 1600, but we have no idea whether these figures represent change or stasis unless we supplement them with figures from another period.

Now turn to Briggs and read pp.6–10 and pp.33–62 and consider what he says in relation to what you have just read in Coward.

Exercise   1   What social orders does each historian identify ? (You may like to list the orders in two columns).

2   What similarities and differences do you note between the social orders of France and England?

3   What similarities and differences do you note in each historian's account ?

Discussion   1   My two columns look something like this, bearing in mind that both writers stress that the divisions between the orders are not clear-cut and that there is not necessarily a direct correspondence between groups of people in the different countries.

France	**England**
Peasantry and vagrants	Labourers and vagrants
Richer peasants, either with independent land holdings or larger tenancies	Husbandmen Yeomen, freeholders and tenants with larger land holdings
Royal officials and judges	
Noblesse de robe/nobles of the robe, lawyers and royal officials who had purchased noble status and its privileges (notably tax exemptions)	Members of the professions
	Gentry
Noblesse d'épée/nobles of the sword, the traditional hereditary nobility	Nobility
Merchants	Merchants
Craftsmen	Craftsmen
Urban poor	Urban poor
Clergy	Clergy

2   As similarities I would suggest the importance of landowning as a measure of status, the fact that distinctions between several of the groups were fairly fluid, but that in general social mobility was restricted.

As differences I would note that the term peasantry is not used of England. Briggs does not define his use of the term, but it is usually used to indicate the occupier of a small parcel of land with attached to it obligations to a seigneur or overlord, which might be exacted in the form of labour or payments in kind or money. These payments were not simply rent (though as the century progressed they came to resemble it) but were part of a system of feudal obligations. In a few regions, ancient seigneurial powers over the peasant's person endured – peasants might not leave their landholding or marry without the seigneur's permission. English country dwellers might occupy land either as tenants or as freeholders without such encumbrances.

The English gentry in some ways resembled the lesser country nobility in France, their economic status was similar. However the English gentry were represented in the House of Commons whilst the French nobility, however poor, were part of the second (noble) estate; we shall discuss this further on pp.17–18. There were, however, similarities between the great nobility in both countries: their closeness to the monarch, their separate assemblies (the House of Lords and the second estate).

There was no English equivalent to the *noblesse de robe*, the royal officials in the *parlements* and other law courts who had bought their offices (I shall say more about this later) and acquired noble status. Most were trained as lawyers, though there were some former merchants. Purchasable offices were real jobs, a few were sinecures but they brought with them the all-important coat of arms and tax exemptions. The highest of the *noblesse de robe* had a good deal in common with the *noblesse d'épée*.

3   Both authors stress the importance of social divisions in the period and the significance of land owning. Both discuss the social orders in terms of economic status as well as in terms of seventeenth-century attitudes to status (Briggs's account is almost entirely related to economic status except for pp.55–8.) Both also stress the difficulties involved in using the term 'class' to describe different social orders in the seventeenth century (Briggs pp.56–7; Coward p.43).

Coward's account differs from Briggs's in that it is much more detailed, much more concerned with specific examples and with illustrating his points with seventeenth-century quotations. He emphasizes the methodology of the historian more specifically than Briggs. Briggs gives us a much more schematic account and raises issues of long-term change untouched on by Coward.

The period and the places

The time-span we have chosen for this course (1620–1714) is conventionally known amongst historians as the early modern period (in fact this is usually considered to begin in the late fifteenth century). It is the period between the decline of the feudal societies and the start of industrialization, the process which initiated modern capitalist societies. Feudal societies were based upon a complicated system of mutual obligation embracing all levels of society from the monarch to the poorest subject. Such obligations survived only in a vestigial form in England but in France seigneurial jurisdictions were widespread and, especially in northern France, influential. Seigneurs (nobles, churchmen, abbots) administered the rights to access to much land in return for various forms of service and payments. Seigneurs often had their own courts and considerable powers over their tenants.

During the seventeenth century France emerged as a unitary state with centralized institutions; during the same period the British Isles developed a constitution much of which is still in place in the United Kingdom. These developments allowed both countries to emerge in the eighteenth century as great powers, though for rather different reasons. So, many of the changes at which we shall be looking might be regarded as a form of modernization, sweeping aside the relics of medieval feudal societies. However, it is possible to see the seventeenth century as the end of an old era just as much as the beginning of a new one. We shall be looking at the thesis that the civil wars in France and the British Isles were struggles to preserve a disappearing order as much as the attempt of new men to gain access to political power.

Why the years 1620 and 1714 in particular? These dates are really historians' shorthand for the assumption of government by the young Louis XIII in France (1617) and the death of King James VI and I of Scotland and England, and the accession of his son Charles I (1625) at the beginning of the period and the deaths of Louis XIV (1715) and of Queen Anne (1714) at the end of the period.

We resolved in planning this course to give Scotland, Ireland and Wales more than the token page or two they usually receive in courses and text books based on early modern England. However, the focus of the course, the formation of the state, is actually more significant in England than in the other countries of the British Isles. If we were to start with Scotland and Ireland our subject would be more likely to be lord-ship and patronage than state formation. Wales is in a slightly different position since its government was integrated with England's from the early sixteenth century and its MPs sat at Westminster. The different histories of Scotland and Ireland mean that some of the concerns of the course, the development of financial institutions for example, have less relevance to them than they have to England. Other concerns, such as popular movements and religious developments, were more important in Scotland and Ireland than they were in England and occupied much government attention.

The terminology of the course title is not in accord with recent usage in Ireland, where the term 'these islands' is used in preference to the 'British Isles'. However, since there are students of Open University course material who come from and who study in many different parts of the world, the term 'these islands' did not seem very satisfactory: there are many archipelagos in other continents.

Princes and peoples: some definitions

In our comparison of France and the British Isles we shall be concentrating upon the course of the seventeenth century. In this section I want to draw your attention to some terms which we shall be using throughout A220.

Princes and peoples: rulers and ruled

The course title, *Princes and Peoples*, indicates that we shall be looking at the relationship between governors and governed in the respective countries. But who were the governors? At the beginning of the period both the kings of France and the British Isles regarded themselves as entitled to exercise absolute power, though in practice their ability to do so was restricted by all sorts of people and bodies.

People who were entitled to exercise power under the monarch (though sometimes against him or her) were generally nobles, commonly their power derived from close contact with the monarchy and from royal patronage. But noblemen and noblewomen exercised their own patronage over others and might derive considerable power from their territorial holdings. Churchmen might also exercise political power but usually did so as a result of their connections with the monarchy. Rich commoners, by providing the monarchy with funds, often acquired great personal influence, influence which might be recognized by a grant of noble status. Bodies which might exercise power for or against the monarch were representative assemblies, urban corporations, law courts and the church. We shall look at these institutions in more detail below.

Some individuals had princely powers, notably princes of the blood (the French king's close relations) and officials like provincial governors in France and the Lord Lieutenant or Deputy Lieutenant of Ireland. The strength of royal power dictated the extent to which such individuals exercised their powers on behalf of, rather than in opposition to, the monarchy.

The governed, the majority of the population, were normally only able to challenge royal power by means of membership of a corporate body or by force. Access to political rights was extremely restricted; all women and the majority of men were excluded from representative bodies and legal corporations and might only use the law courts to a limited extent.

Absolutism

We shall be considering the relationship between governors and governed in terms of the development of absolutism in the state. The word 'absolutism' was not used in the seventeenth century; it was first used in the late eighteenth century, in the period of the French Revolution, though the adjective 'absolute' was used earlier by political theorists as in 'absolute power' or 'absolute government'. Sometimes the term is used to describe a political philosophy, sometimes as a form of political system, and sometimes is a synonym for the entire *ancien régime* (the social and political system overthrown at the French Revolution). Some historians assume that the end of absolutism is absolute power, others argue that it represents a form of political power which contains its own limitations and restrictions. You will find that different authors will use the term in different senses.

Monarchs might aspire to absolute rule but in both France and the British Isles there were important, though different, limitations on the monarch's freedom of action. Absolutism, then, as a term used by historians, does not simply mean unlimited powers vested in a single person. It refers as much to the aspirations of the monarchy as to its achievements. The justification for a monarch exercising absolute power was developed by such sixteenth-century political theorists as Jean Bodin who argued also that the divine origins of monarchial power prevented it from becoming a tyranny because the monarch remained accountable to God.

Divine right

This doctrine, the divine right of monarchy, was taken up by King James VI of Scotland who wrote a treatise, *The True Law of Free Monarchies*, published in 1598, in which he argued that the king was above the law and 'betwixt the king and his people God is doubtless the only judge'. In a speech made in 1610, after he had succeeded to the throne of England, he articulated the doctrine more fully, 'kings are not only God's lieutenants on earth, and sit upon God's throne, but even by God himself they are called gods' (Hughes, 1980, pp.27–8). His son, Charles I, was an enthusiastic subscriber. 'I owe an account of my actions to none but God alone' (Gardiner, 1906, p.73), is a characteristic statement of his views.

The state

Unlike the term 'absolutism' the term 'the state' was widely used in the seventeenth century. It is uncertain whether Louis XIV ever said 'l'état c'est moi' (I am the State), but 'state' was certainly a term used by Cardinal Richelieu. In a letter to Louis XIII in 1628 he wrote, 'in capturing La Rochelle your Majesty has ended what has been the most glorious undertaking for yourself and the most useful one for your state in your lifetime' (Bonney, 1988, p.9). Here Richelieu seems to be using the term 'state' in a sense equivalent to nation. The term is used in a more restricted sense in 1626 in the English parliamentary articles for impeaching the Duke of Buckingham, 'the said Duke, being young and inexperienced, hath of late years, with exorbitant ambition and for his own profit and advantage, procured and engrossed into his own hands the said several offices … to the danger of the state' (Gardiner, 1906, p.8).

The term 'state' at best embodies a rather nebulous concept and is most easily defined in relation to its responsibilities and institutions. Why, then, do we need such a concept? Such a concept allows us to understand that there are important but invisible relationships between the institutions which organize society. It acts upon society but it is not separate from it. The state has the responsibility of maintaining order, of defending the country against aggressors, and of protecting people and property, and controls the institutions by which it seeks to achieve these things. But it plainly isn't enough to define the state in terms of its institutions, as opposed to its responsibilities, as these are very culture- and time-specific. The existence of institutions is, as it were, only the circumstantial evidence of the existence of the state. The most important function of the state is to defend itself, after that perhaps it is to provide the links between the responsibilities and the institutions which carry out those responsibilities.

I have used a minimalist definition of the state, concentrating on its responsibilities, but it is actually very difficult to think of the state in such restricted terms. Let us turn now to a more highly developed definition. Read Offprint 1 (pp.5–6).

Exercise   How does Aylmer characterize the state?

Discussion   Aylmer uses a much more sophisticated definition drawn from sociological literature. His basic definition includes institutions and personnel, emphasizes coercion and draws attention to geography. In looking at the effects of the state on the governed he brings in ideology and finances.

Nation

We shall consider the institutions of the state and its financial functions below (pp.16–26). Here we shall look at the geographical aspects of the state. We have seen how Cardinal Richelieu used the term 'state' to embrace what we would describe as a nation, a geographical entity and its people. The term 'nation' was in the seventeenth century more likely to be used in a sense equivalent to region. Cardinal Mazarin's foundation, the *Collège de Quatre Nations* (the College of Four Nations), was for sixty gentlemen from the four provinces ceded to France under the Treaty of Münster in 1648 (Artois, Alsace, Roussillon and Piedmont).

In 1620 France was clearly a state within Aylmer's terms, but it was certainly not a single nation. Briggs (p.2) describes how the kingdom grew during the later middle ages and the sixteenth century by a slow process of accretion. The king ruled over a very diverse country, perhaps best described as a composite kingdom, made up of a variety of regions some of which had well-developed and idiosyncratic local institutions, prepared to assert their regional or jurisdictional rights against what they saw as the centralizing tendencies of the French crown. In addition, under the terms of the Edict of Nantes (1598) (see Briggs pp.30–1), Protestants were given rights of self government in a number of cities, such as La Rochelle and Nantes itself. In the distinct privileges which provinces and Protestants had, they saw their guarantee of freedom.

The British Isles, though ruled by a single person, were not a single nation. All the Stuart monarchs until 1707 were separately rulers of England and Wales, Scotland and Ireland. A useful term for this is multiple kingdom. The accretion of kingdoms certainly enhanced the monarch's power and created a larger power-base in Europe, but these kingdoms did not create a single state, except to the extent that English foreign policy became dominant, and they certainly remained separate nations, as they are today.

Religion

Aylmer suggests that important elements of the state are 'a monopoly of rule making' and that the state 'may indoctrinate, inculcate, or at a minimum merely provide a kind of protective covering for dominant groups or classes to do this within its boundaries'. This suggests that the state has the power to control what ideas were disseminated, especially in relation to itself. In modern states we see this aspect most commonly in secular matters associated with censorship or with discrimination against certain groups. However, one of the absolutely essential differences between France and the British Isles today and in the seventeenth century is in the matter of religion. In the context of the early modern state, religion was virtually the only ideology which mattered.

As Coward says (p.127), 'One cannot exaggerate just how seriously contemporaries considered the threat which refusal to accept the legally established church posed to the state'. Religion provided subjects with a higher authority than the monarch, thus only obedience to the religion of the monarch could ensure real obedience to the state. The desire for uniformity, for government over subjects' consciences, lies behind much royal policy in the seventeenth century, though rulers were often prepared to settle for the outward forms of religion, recognizing that they could not rule their subjects' souls.

In France attempts to establish Protestantism had led to thirty years of civil war, the sixteenth-century Wars of Religion. The settlement secured by the Huguenots in 1598 under the Edict of Nantes proved to be a fragile one. However, while it lasted Protestants had considerable privileges, for it was only by possessing privileges that they could have the freedom to practise their religion. The government of France was in the hands of churchmen, but it was their concern for political stability rather than their consciences which led them to oppose the Huguenots. In 1625 Richelieu wrote to Louis XIII, pointing to the complexity of the relations between state and religion:

> As for the Huguenots, they are accustomed to advance their cause at the expense of the state, and to seize their opportunity when they see us occupied against those who are our declared enemies. As long as the Huguenots have a foothold in France, the king will never be master at home. (Bonney, 1988, p.5)

And a few months later he wrote:

> It is certain that as long as the Huguenot party exists in France, the king will not be absolute in his kingdom, and he will not be able to establish the order and rule to which his conscience obliges him and which the necessity of his people requires. (Bonney, 1988, p.7)

There are parallels between the attitude of the French monarchy to Protestantism and that of the English monarchy to Roman Catholicism. Roman Catholics in England were believed to give their first allegiance to the pope rather than the monarch, hence the association between Roman Catholicism and treason. The Oath of Allegiance to the crown required subjects to swear:

> ... that the pope neither of himself nor by any authority of the church or of Rome, or by any other means with any other, hath any power to depose the king, ... or to discharge any of his subjects of their allegiance and obedience to his majesty. (Dures, 1983, p.98)

However, an important difference between France and England is that whereas Protestantism was officially tolerated in France in the places specified in the Edict of Nantes, nowhere was Roman Catholicism tolerated in England, though the severity with which Catholics were persecuted fluctuated considerably.

Attempts to create a Protestant state in Ireland were doomed to failure. The majority of the population (the Gaelic Irish) was Roman Catholic and attempts to proselytize it were generally not successful. James I at first accepted this and commented that 'though he would much rejoice if the Irish Catholics would conform themselves to his religion, yet he would not force them to forsake their own' (Moody, Martin and Byrne, 1978, p.190). However, this soft approach was not to last and when the Catholic descendants of the English settlers of the twelfth century, known as Old English, went to see James in 1614 to protest their loyalty to him, he replied, 'I have good reason for saying that you are only half-subjects of mine' (Moody, Martin, and Byrne, 1978, p.217). And there was a further problem in Ireland for there were two quite separate Protestant churches. There was the Church of Ireland, established after the Henrician reformation and in communion with the Church of England, whose members were chiefly English settlers and their descendants. There was the Presbyterian church, established in the early seventeenth century when Scottish settlers began to arrive in Ulster and in communion with the Presbyterian Church of Scotland.

Here we see one of the anomalies in the British monarchy as head of four separate churches, one of which was theologically quite different from the other three. Conformity to the Presbyterian Church of Scotland was well established in central, southern and north-east Scotland. Only in the sparsely populated western Highlands were there many traces of Roman Catholicism. Distance, lack of ministers, and the persistence of clan disorder meant that little attention was given to Catholics by the government in Edinburgh, though fear of Roman Catholicism remained a force in politics. Turn now to the *Anthology* (I.1).

Exercise What view of the Scottish nation does this Scots writer set forth?

Discussion For David Calderwood the nation is indistinguishable from its religion and Scotland was peculiarly blessed in its discovery of the light of the gospel. This was not an unusual view for the seventeenth century and carried with it the belief, which dominated policy-making within the country, that the function of the state was to support a godly commonwealth. Religion was to be furthered by the secular power.

Language

The cultural and national elements of the state are combined in its language. In 1620 French was the language of government, the law courts and of official business, but probably a majority of people spoke other languages – Breton, Flemish, Occitanian, Catalan or Basque – or French dialects. In England a variety of dialects were spoken and Welsh was widely used in Wales. Latin and legal French were used for some official business but were increasingly being replaced by English. A more standardized form of English was spreading through Scotland and Ireland although there were substantial areas where Gaelic was spoken.

Before proceeding, you should work on AC 1, section 1 in which I look at the geography, economies and population distribution of France and the British Isles in the early seventeenth century. You will need, in addition to the audio-cassette, the Illustration Book. This exercise should take about 30 minutes.

The state and its workings

In this section we look at the bodies which performed the functions of the state, in Aylmer's words the 'set of institutions with its own personnel, including the means of violence and coercion': the monarchy, assemblies of subjects and law courts. We shall then look at the administration of the provinces and finally at the state's finances. But first, what is the relationship between the state and the government? The government is the agency which performs many of the functions of the state, but in the seventeenth century some state functions now carried out by governments were performed by other bodies or groups of people. The most important element in the government was the monarchy.

The institutions of the state

The monarchy

One of the phrases often used of the French monarchy is that the king of France was emperor in his own kingdom. By this is meant that he owed allegiance to no higher power, neither the Holy Roman Emperor, nor the papacy. The king of England, Scotland and Ireland similarly lacked an overlord. However, it is also clear that the monarchy by itself did not constitute the whole of the power in the state despite the aspirations of some monarchs. The constitutional position of the English king was that he ruled as, 'the king in Parliament' and in all the countries it was questionable whether the king, the fount of all justice, was actually above the law.

Turn now to Coward and read pp.91–5 and 119–24 and to Briggs and read pp.27–32 and pp.76–84.

Exercise   What was the extent of the monarch's power in France and England?

Discussion   In both countries the monarch had considerable powers, but their full extent was ill-defined and rarely tested. However, a very great deal hung on the monarch's personality, and there was little distinction between the person and the office of king. A strong king might stretch his powers, Briggs writes of Henri IV's 'frequent and arbitrary interventions in the affairs of towns and provinces' (p.80). And the weakness of the French monarchy in the years following Henri's death owed much to the deficiencies of Marie de Medici as regent. The personalities of James I and Charles I also played a critical part in the successes and failures of the English monarchy in the early seventeenth century.

The king conducted foreign policy and appointed ministers. The royal bureaucracy or civil service were his personal servants. Royal councils were the chief bodies for executing royal policy. Both kings appointed provincial officials, but the potential advantages to the king of France were diminished by the effect of the sale of offices (see below, pp.23–5).

The king was also responsible for calling and dissolving assemblies. The French Estates General, the national assembly of clergy, nobles and commoners, was called in 1614 and was not to meet again until the eighteenth century. The parliaments of England, Scotland and Ireland met more frequently but the king was not required to call them at any particular interval.

The extent of the king's powers was similar, though not identical, in England and Wales, Scotland and Ireland. The king was sovereign in Scotland though, after the union of the crowns in 1603, Scotland ceased to have an independent foreign policy. The king of England had been declared king of Ireland in 1541 and Ireland was technically a sovereign kingdom under the direction of a Lord or Deputy Lieutenant appointed by the king and assisted by a council.

The most important area of royal initiative was a loosely defined right called the 'prerogative' under which the king might do certain things purely on the basis that he was the king. Louis XIII suspended the provincial estates (the local assembly of clergy, nobles and commoners) in Dauphiné under this right and the king of England dispensed individuals from the operation of the law.

But to return to the basic functions of the state (protection of persons and property, defence against aggressors and maintenance of order), it is clear that neither the king of France nor the king of England had the power to do all these things without the participation of other bodies in the kingdom. Monarchs appointed judges (in the case of France only to a limited extent since the offices were sold); were heads of the army and navy and might assemble them at will (though this right was beginning to be contested in England); appointed many of the people who executed royal policy (though, again, in France subject to the operation of sales). The two things which neither monarch could do unaided, though both attempted it, were to make laws and to raise all the money necessary for royal administration.

Assemblies

Turn to Briggs pp.6, 91–2, 95 and to Coward pp.101–3, and 108–10.

Exercise   What functions did assemblies have in France and England?

Discussion   The chief function of the French estates was to authorize taxation. They did not draw up or approve legislation, though they might present lists of grievances – *cahiers de doléances* – to the king. The English parliament secured 'legislation and the resolution of grievances' (Coward p.102) and it voted taxation, increasingly important as the king found it more difficult to meet the ordinary expenses of government.

Parliament, consisting of the House of Lords and the House of Commons, initiated legislation but all legislation required the approval of both houses of parliament and the royal assent. Conscious of the king's requirements for money, parliament challenged the king's prerogative powers, especially the appointment of ministers and the conduct of foreign policy. Parliament also had the power to grant the king the right to collect certain taxes. At his succession it traditionally granted him, for life, the income from some of the customs dues, for example tunnage and poundage. It also granted him the right to collect assessments for specific purposes, normally wars.

The English parliament had no jurisdiction over the parliaments of Scotland and Ireland. Ireland had a bi-cameral legislature; Scotland a single chamber, though the General Assembly of the kirk might be likened to the clerical chamber of the French Estates General. The Scottish parliament met infrequently and briefly, granted taxation, passed legislation and sought to resolve disputes between members. It had no permanent meeting place until 1639. The Irish parliament likewise met infrequently and its jurisdiction, although technically covering all Ireland, in fact extended only to the counties round Dublin. It was not subject to the English parliament, but its business had to be approved by the Lord or Deputy Lieutenant and his council in Dublin and by the monarch and his or her council in London.

The French Estates General, the national assembly consisting of the three estates of clergy, nobles and commoners, did not meet at all during the period 1620–1714. However, the provincial estates, the clergy, nobles and commoners of certain provinces, did meet. Not all provinces had estates, but in those that did the estates voted the assessment of the chief direct tax, the *taille*. The provincial estates were fiercely protective of their rights, despite royal attempts to restrict them. In 1628 a royal edict imposed a new financial structure on the province of Dauphiné which allowed the collection of the *taille* without reference to the Dauphiné estates. There was fierce opposition, but by 1639 the new system had been set in place under the direction of an *intendant*, a high-ranking civil servant appointed from Paris. Similar attempts by the crown to remove the control of the *taille* from provincial estates were made in Burgundy, Languedoc and Provence. But in these provinces the three estates were more united against royal encroachments than they were in Dauphiné. By making a large payment to the crown, they bought back the right to approve *taille* levies. This suggests that the aim of the policy was to increase crown revenue rather than reform provincial administration.

The individual estates in the provinces, the clergy, nobility, and commoners, sometimes met as separate assemblies not constituted as estates. In Provence in 1639 the provincial estates were replaced by an 'assembly of communities'. There were also assemblies of smaller districts, groups of parishes and inhabitants. Local communities of parishes or groups of hamlets were run by assemblies which met in a public place between six and sixteen times a year, and organized the assessment and collection of taxes, the maintenance of order, the upkeep of church, roads and bridges and the administration of common land. Such assemblies made regulations for the community and might make representations over grievances to assemblies or officials at a higher level.

Both France and the British Isles had urban corporations, bodies which regulated trade, building roads and so on in towns and cities. Most were governed by an assembly of some kind which might be elected on a broad or narrow franchise. Towns were fiercely protective of their rights which often included considerable powers to raise money from taxes and such sources as market dues.

Law courts

Kings appointed judges (in France only the most senior judicial appointments were not purchasable) and were the fount of all justice. But the extent to which the administration of justice was under the king's control is highly debatable.

The royal courts in France used Roman or civil law (as was used in Scotland but not in England, Wales or Ireland). There were numerous other courts with different jurisdictions: seigneurial courts, church courts, and courts with specialized functions in different provinces. The most important courts were the *parlements* (which were not representative assemblies) and of these the pre-eminent court was the Paris *parlement* whose jurisdiction covered much of northern France. *Parlements* in other regions had similar functions: they registered royal edicts (providing a check on royal legislative powers) and might present what were known as 'remonstrances' to the king, indicating constitutional or legal difficulties with a proposed edict. The king might ignore these remonstrances.

Parlements combined a fierce defence of regional and sectional rights with being a royal agency in the provinces. Roland Mousnier has described this tension well:

> ... in general every body of royal officials had to show fealty and therefore obedience to the king, but these magistrates owed to their consciences respect for their professional integrity and therefore had to refuse to obey orders that ran counter to this integrity. They owed respect to the dignity of justice and therefore had to maintain just relations between the king and his subjects, which meant, if need be, protecting subjects from their king. (Mousnier, 1979, p.609)

The more senior *parlementaires* had acquired noble status with the purchase of their offices. Now turn to Briggs and read pp.96–9.

Exercise   How did the crown seek to limit the powers of the *parlements*?

Discussion   The crown reduced the rewards and status of royal officials by exacting payments from officials, it set up new courts to diminish the influence of the *parlements*, and increased the number of officers.

Parlements potentially had more power to obstruct the king than provincial assemblies by being able to hold up taxation and the registration of royal edicts. Louis XIII complained to the *parlement* of Paris in 1627

> I cannot think ... that my court of *parlement* took full account of the consequences for my affairs. I will leave on one side the attack on decrees of my council which were issued to carry out my edicts ... By trying to delay the enforcement of these edicts and to prohibit my judges from carrying out my commission, my court of *parlement* makes itself arbiter of the obedience which should be rendered to my commands by my officeholders and subjects ... I cannot be considered as subordinate to a body which has power and existence only as a result of my own authority. (Bonney, 1988, pp.94–5)

As the embodiment of provincial liberties they were also able to draw on considerable local loyalty, though it has also to be said that their defence of their privileges did not always endear them to the local population.

English law courts had less scope for independent action. Lawyers and law officers were important, but many members of parliament were lawyers and while parliament sat, used that as a means of seeking remedies for grievances. It was when parliament was not sitting that the courts were used for testing the legality of the king's actions. In 1627 the legality of forced loans was tested in the Five Knight's case and in 1637–8 John Hampden tested the legality of ship money (see Coward pp.162, 168–9). The early Stuart kings themselves sought to reinforce policies of dubious legality by their use of the prerogative court of Star Chamber. Many of the prosecutions there were associated with the failure of officials to enforce unpopular policies.

In Ireland, English common law was used in the courts set up by the administration in Dublin and, to a large extent, they were the agency of English rule. It is difficult to tell how far their power extended beyond the counties round Dublin. By contrast, the Scottish legal profession was fiercely defensive of its own standing not least because it practised Roman and not common law. But the courts were nevertheless used to crush dissent to royal rule, as in the case of Lord Balmerino in 1634 (see Coward p.179).

The state in the provinces

Both England and France retained relics of a provincial administration which was based on military requirements in the lord and deputy lieutenants of the English shires and in the provincial governorships in France. Lord and deputy lieutenancies were, by the seventeenth century, not particularly influential offices in contrast to the French provincial governorships. Governorships were always filled by nobles, often princes of the blood, and brought with them a considerable amount of patronage. They built up clientèles amongst the provincial nobility and distributed patronage – posts and pensions – creating power blocs and acting as brokers of royal patronage.

The provincial government of England was fairly stable in this period, while that of France not only differed from province to province, but was also in the process of great change. Read Coward pp.96–100.

Exercise   From what you have read already about France, how would you compare the provincial government of the two countries?

Discussion   Much the most striking points are:

1   the absence of assemblies in English local government and their ubiquity in France;

2   the reliance upon part-time, semi-amateur officers appointed from the local gentry to run English local government. In France officers were paid professionals, increasingly appointed from Paris to the non-purchasable office of *intendant.*

The local governments of Scotland and Ireland more closely resembled England than France, though in both countries there were substantial areas which were relatively untouched by royal government, notably the Scottish Highlands and Connaught in the west of Ireland. In both countries too, attempts were made to develop local government by justices of the peace. In Ireland this was largely unsuccessful except in the counties immediately round Dublin. In Scotland, justices were introduced in 1609 but with restricted powers which impinged little upon the many independent noble jurisdictions.

Royal finances

In this section of the unit we shall see how rulers raised money to support their government and how the ruled responded to the demands made of them.

The king's income

Although it was believed in both England and France that the monarch should meet the expenses of government out of the revenues from his private lands (and in England he was granted certain taxes for his reign), it was becoming increasingly clear that monarchs could not run government out of ordinary income, even if no special demands were made of it. In Scotland royal revenue had ceased to keep the king and his government before James VI succeeded the throne of England in 1603. Guests at royal banquets in Scotland had even had to take their own food. The Scottish economy was much less prosperous than that of England and the principal source of revenue was the customs dues. Further occasional taxes levied on the rural population, which consisted chiefly of subsistence farmers, could never raise much revenue. The taxation levied in Ireland was intended to support the English government there, though there was a considerable deficit, of perhaps as much as £20,000 a year, which the government in Dublin tried to overcome, usually by the expedient of increasing fines on Roman Catholics. The kings' inability to support their ordinary activities had a variety of causes. Read Briggs pp.84–109 and re-read Coward pp.108–10.

Exercise Why were the two monarchies unable to meet their commitments from their normal income?

Discussion Both countries were faced with price rises which diminished the value of income from royal lands. In England royal revenue fell by a quarter during James I's reign after sales of crown lands to meet debts. Taxes were often administered in such a way that when the income did increase it went to someone other than the king. So there were a number of structural reasons why the income from taxes failed to keep up with the costs of government. There were also reasons more specific to times, places and personalities. James I was notoriously extravagant; both countries underwent substantial periods of war; and France had a considerable period of internal turmoil which made taxes difficult to collect.

Royal revenue needed to be increased and in both England and France this was done by exploiting existing mechanisms not by changing the tax system. Opposition to taxation in England seems usually to have taken the form of challenging the right of the king to levy it. Such challenges were generally mounted in the law courts by relatively rich and influential individuals. Since raising new taxes was generally done under the royal prerogative such cases were a serious matter. In 1606 a merchant called John Bate had refused to pay an additional charge on imported currants, the judge found against him. Read the *Anthology* (I.2), the judgement passed on the case.

Exercise   What reasons did the judge give for his judgement?

Discussion   The judge argued that the king was entitled to levy this charge under his extraordinary power. All customs were the product of foreign trade and all dealings with foreigners were governed by the king. Such trade could only take place through ports controlled by the king and protected by him as he protected merchants at sea with the navy and travellers abroad by his envoys ('they are to be relieved if they are oppressed by foreign princes ...'). This is a pretty comprehensive invocation of all the monarch's responsibilities to justify the exercise of one of his powers. In particular, the argument draws upon the notion that Bate the subject is different from Bate the merchant.

Note that although the king was granted customs dues for life, the judge raises the question of parliament's permission.

Bate was a merchant and, in general, until the 1630s, most challenges to taxation in England were connected with trade. The decline in trade, especially in the cloth manufacturing districts, produced numerous petitions to the crown to alleviate the economically distressed workers, as well as petitions protesting the burden of taxation. From Lincolnshire came in 1621 a petition asking that less money be demanded because of 'the strange alteration and delay both of our rents, commodities and estates which have generally befallen us these two or three years' (Thirsk and Cooper, 1972, p.608).

Challenges to taxation took a rather different form in France. Read Briggs pp.109–18 and the *Anthology* (I.3).

Exercise   How was opposition to taxation expressed in France?

Discussion   To a large extent, by popular disturbances. Briggs suggests that the vast majority of revolts were demonstrations involving minor public order offences and were regarded as a legitimate form of popular political action. It was the collectors of the taxes who were attacked rather than the more abstract system which allowed the tax to be levied. However, not all opposition was controlled. The level of violence in Agen is very striking. The riot started suddenly and resulted both in violence against persons and against property.

Types of tax

The two main types of tax were direct taxes, money payments exacted from subjects directly by the crown on the basis of some rough kind of assessment, and indirect taxes, levied on sales, transfers or transport of goods or services or on industrial processes, and paid on the goods. However, most direct taxes were occasional, levied to meet specific demands and often only on certain classes of people.

The most important direct tax in France was the *taille*. It was levied on land which was designated noble or commoner. In the north of France nobles were exempt regardless of whether they occupied noble or commoner estates and commoners had to pay even if they occupied noble estates. This was known as the *taille personelle*. In the south of France nobles occupying commoner estates had to pay the *taille*; this was known as the *taille réelle*. To raise its income the crown sought to increase the number of people assessed for the *taille réelle*. This it did by reducing the areas where taxes were administered by provincial estates and substituting for the estates the finance courts run by royal officials known as *élections*. Such a manoeuvre was achieved in Dauphiné in the 1630s where the provincial estates were suspended and the administration taken over by royal officials, *intendants* and *élus*.

There were many more indirect taxes in France than in England, but they made up only about a quarter of the French crown's revenue in the first half of the seventeenth century. The *aides*, internal customs dues levied especially on drink, were the most important indirect tax, but the most unpopular was the *gabelle*, a tax on salt.

England also had direct and indirect taxes. Most of the direct taxes were subsidies, voted by parliament as extraordinary revenue and levied by county on the basis of local valuations. The chief indirect taxes were various forms of customs dues levied on imports to and exports from abroad, some of which were granted to the king for life. There were no internal customs as there were in France though there were some customs duties between the different parts of the British Isles. There were also a few feudal dues. Efforts to abolish these and replace them with new levels of customs and excise (the tax paid on alcoholic drinks) in 1610 were not successful.

In Scotland regular taxation was only introduced in 1581 and corresponded with the penetration of the judicial system into the localities. Customs dues were levied by the crown but were considerably lower than those in England. As in England, the Scottish parliament used the grant of taxes as an opportunity for submitting lists of grievances to the king. Each tax was a one-off event and supported only the government of Scotland. In Ireland taxes were raised from customs, from parliamentary subsidies, which were rarely collected outside the Pale, and from the income from royal lands.

It was not only the government, central or local, which levied taxes. All over France and the British Isles there were people and institutions who were entitled to claim labour, goods or money from people. The most important institution able to raise taxes, apart from the state, was the church. The custom of levying a tax of one-tenth of a householder's annual produce to support the clergy survived from the medieval church in both France and England (where the Church of England simply carried on with the pre-Reformation system) and even in Scotland something of the pre-Reformation system survived in *teinds* or tithes.

There were also private individuals who were entitled to levy dues from their tenants. These were the relics of a feudal system where land-holding was part of a system of mutual obligation and protection. This system survived in France, especially in the north, where many local communities had seigneurs. Seigneurs might be resident or non-resident, nobles, wealthy commoners, churchmen or institutions. What is important is that they had jurisdiction over the people who occupied their land. In England these private jurisdictions had substantially disappeared and obligations to labour or military service had usually been commuted to money payments.

I've already suggested that kings had access to other sorts of income than their personal estates or taxes. One source which was particularly important was the sale of royal offices in the central and in the provincial government.

Sales of offices

In France, sales of offices in many areas of the royal administration became widespread from 1522. From 1604 office-holders might pass on their offices in return for a payment to the crown of one-sixtieth of the value of the office. This tax was known as the *droit annuel* or *paulette*. By 1633 returns to the *bureau des parties casuelles*, who administered the tax, made up more than half of the crown's ordinary revenue. Only *intendants* (royal officers in the provinces), *premiers présidents* of the *parlements* and certain officials connected with the royal council did not buy their offices.

The system had the advantage for the monarchy of providing a substantial income which was under its control and which could be increased, and was, by the creation of new offices. Venal office-holders were dependent on the crown not on the clientage of great nobles. The administration of the country was transferred from the clients of great nobles to royal officials. Some of these officials bought their offices, but the most important, the *intendants*, did not.

The advantages were counterweighed by the disadvantage that purchase of an office and the right to pass it on to his heirs gave the incumbent a certain independence of his master. This is very clearly illustrated in 1635 when, following the declaration of war with Spain, Richelieu attempted to create 24 new offices of *conseiller* in the *parlement* of Paris, both to raise money and to devalue the office. This outraged the existing *conseillers* who protested, were arrested and sent into exile. The *Chambre des Enquêtes*, the body which prepared cases and briefed magistrates, then went on strike, bringing the work of the courts to a standstill. Richelieu had then to agree to reduce the number of new *conseillers* to 17 instead of 24.

For office-holders themselves the system had considerable advantages. Once bought, offices were regarded as part of a family's patrimony. An unusually long tenure was that of the Phelypeau family, nine members of which occupied the office of secretary of state between 1610 and 1777, but successions of two or three members of the same family were common.

Despite the increase in the number of offices, their prices rose continuously. The office of *conseiller* in the *parlement* of Paris was bought for 40,000 livres in 1627, the price had risen to 100,000 livres in 1634 and to

120,000 in 1636. The economic effects are difficult to calculate, but there is little doubt that buying offices (and thus noble rank) consumed large amounts of capital.

The size of the English bureaucracy remained small by comparison with that of France. James I's attempts in 1616 to sell offices won him little financial reward and much unpopularity. The English crown never became dependent upon sales of offices as a regular source of revenue, and the profits of the traffic in offices to a large extent simply redistributed wealth within the ruling class who bought and sold offices between them. The king was only one among many who received the purchase price, or a portion of it. Senior officials, the previous incumbent, or his heirs, or a royal favourite or minister might also be entitled to money for offices. The sums involved were large. Sir Henry Montagu is said to have paid £15,000 in 1616 to be made Lord Justice and in 1620 he paid a further £20,000 (probably in the guise of a loan to the king) to be promoted to Lord Treasurer. One of the chief complaints against the Duke of Buckingham was for his activities as broker in negotiating admission to offices in return for a fee.

In the English parliaments of the 1620s sales of offices were not identified as a specific grievance but were sometimes mentioned in complaints about sales of peerages. Any attack on the sales of offices in England would, in any case, have lacked a certain force since many of the lawyers who were MPs held purchasable offices. Indeed, there is evidence to suggest that fewer offices were sold during the 1630s than earlier, and that the king did not profit from those that were sold. Few common law judges, except for Irish appointments, paid for their positions and purchase even became unusual for appointments in the royal household. Gerald Aylmer, historian of Charles I's civil service, argues that there was more of a decline in the sales of offices in the highest ranks of government than in the middle and lower ranks, amongst central than local appointments and among English appointments more than Irish (Aylmer, 1974, p.233). However, though sales were not used to raise revenue for the crown, ways were found of exacting revenue from office-holders, fining them for alleged abuses, for example.

Tax collectors and farmers

In England direct taxes were usually collected by parish constables or churchwardens and passed on to commissioners, local gentlemen acting as agents of the crown. It was the relative inefficiency of this system which led to the assessment and collection of ship money being transferred to county sheriffs in the 1630s. Collectors usually had the power to distrain on defaulters' possessions. In France village communities generally administered the assessment and collection of taxes; collectors had powers to enforce payment. The money was passed on to royal officials in the *pays d'élections* and to officers of the provincial estates in the *pays d'état*. Payment of seigneurial dues was the responsibility of the seigneur's bailiff and payment might be enforced in the seigneurial court.

But many taxes, especially indirect taxes, were collected by people who were not officers of the state at all. Such taxes were collected by 'farmers', private individuals who leased the right from the crown to collect a particular tax for a specified period. Tax farmers were extremely unpopular because they were regarded as profiting from people's misfortune. In France the clerks responsible on behalf of the tax farmers for collecting the *gabelle* (the tax on salt) and the excise lived in some danger. In Saint Benoist sur Mer in 1633 the *gabelleur* (collector of the *gabelle*) was hanged and his dismembered body displayed round the region. By 1644 peasant riots against the *gabelle* were so common that the farmers were allowed to levy two companies of fusiliers at the crown's expense, to enforce payment.

The commissioners for excise (government officials responsible for collecting the tax on alcoholic drinks) in England in 1656 wrote to the Council of State asking that the tax be collected by tax collectors rather than farmers. They said that taxpayers felt that the tax collected by an official was for the public good, but when collected by a farmer it was for private profit. The excise on beer had to be collected directly from brewers who, the commissioners said, were an influential and wealthy group of men, but 'rough and surly', 'contentious and forward', and they did not want to have all their time taken up by complaints from them.

Both France and England used tax farmers, but the success of their endeavours differed markedly. In early seventeenth-century France the combination of overvaluing the potential revenue with a succession of poor harvests, subsistence crises, plague, foreign wars and domestic upheavals meant that the yield was often less than the ostensible value of leases. Those on whom the taxes fell most heavily, the commoners, suffered most from natural disasters. To appease the tax farmers, and forestall their financial failure, the government compensated them when tax revenues were down. So, certainly in the early seventeenth century, the collection of taxes in France by farmers was an extremely uneconomic way of raising revenue. Farmers were commonly financiers with wider interests and were expected to advance money to the king, anticipating income from farms, becoming bankers to the government as well as tax collectors.

In England fewer taxes were farmed but those that were, as for example customs duties and taxes on wine and currants, provided a much more stable income than the farmed taxes in France. As in France, tax farmers also made loans to the crown, usually fairly short-term loans anticipating the revenues from the farm for a couple of years. It has been suggested that in England tax farms were almost seen as a reward for bankers who had served the crown's borrowing requirements well.

Although tax farmers in both France and England employed their own agents they were entitled to draw on the resources of the state to enforce payment. In France, as we have seen, farmers and sub-farmers might use troops raised by the state in really difficult cases, but there was also a whole system of law courts, the *cours des aides*, whose primary function was to try cases resulting from the administration of the chief direct and indirect taxes, including those which were farmed. The farmers of English customs duties might call on the law to enforce payment.

Taxpayers

Very large numbers of people paid taxes, especially in France where people had to be very poor or very privileged to avoid them. In France, nobility and clergy were largely exempt from paying the *taille*, indeed it was regarded as ignoble to pay it and the honour of tax exempt status was much sought after. The most privileged people (and often the richest) paid least tax. So the tax burden fell heavily upon the peasantry who registered their objections by armed revolts.

England and Wales were much less taxed than France, and Scotland and Ireland less than England and Wales. There were no major tax exemptions, but quite poor people might be taxed. There were some anomalies in that it was possible (though unusual) to be simultaneously liable for, and in receipt of, parish relief, though this should not be surprising in that nowadays many people receiving benefits from the state also pay tax. Taxes in the British Isles seem to have been relatively easy to collect, possibly because of their low level. Certainly by comparison with France there were no tax revolts.

Most English taxpayers paid direct taxes as householders on the basis of their occupation of a particular piece of land, though the amount for which they were assessed was not necessarily based upon the value of the land. One widely collected tax in England payable by householders and occupiers of land was the poor rate. This was a tax established under the Elizabethan poor law for the relief of the poor. In towns the system was well established by the seventeenth century. In York in the 1630s about 25 per cent of households paid the poor rate, the proportion rose to about 43 per cent in the 1670s (Slack, 1988, p.177). In the countryside, however, it was not until the 1660s that the poor rate was collected in many rural parishes. The collection of the rate was administered by churchwardens and overseers of the poor in each parish.

Turn now to *Anthology*, I.4.

Exercise   How was the legislation put into effect?

Discussion   The document shows how the poor law statutes were administered 'in his Majesty's name' by two of the justices of the peace in Oxford. They instructed the parish churchwardens and overseers of the poor to levy the poor rate in the parish of St Martin's, giving them the right to collect it forcibly from non-payers. The reference to arrears suggests that they did not exercise their powers over-zealously.

We do not have the list of poor rate payers in St Martin's parish for 1620, but we have one for 1606–8. Fifty-one names appear on the list, including a city alderman, two widows and 'Mrs Williams of the Star' (presumably an inn-keeper). The money was due quarterly, the lowest payment being 1*d* monthly and the highest 6*d* monthly. The collectors used a system for ticking off payments made. Another list, of people in arrears, corresponds with the missing ticks. Alderman Cossom was 1*s* 6*d* (3 months) in arrears in 1606; Mr Francis Harris owed 4*s* for a whole year.

Local taxpayers seem to have been little different in France. The assessment of the *taille* in villages was made in the local assembly which made a list of taxpayers. Householders were liable (though whether they paid as persons or on the basis of the land they occupied depended on whether they lived in a *pays d'état* or a *pays d'élection*). Householders might be women, more commonly widows than single women.

Although relatively few women in France or England were tax-payers, women often played a disproportionately large role in riots about taxes or grain prices. One reason for this is that these were financial matters which affected women deeply as household managers. Another reason is that there was some doubt as to whether women were responsible in law for such breaches of the peace.

The state and society

Let us now return to the broader subject of the nature of the state in the early seventeenth century. The state was able to carry out the basic functions we have delineated, though not necessarily in ways which are readily recognizable today. It was extremely hierarchical, a hierarchy ordained by God.

The notions of an immutable hierarchy ordained by God underlay the thinking of many people in France and the British Isles, chiefly those from the higher social orders. We shall see later on in the course that the orders were not quite as immutable as some contemporaries believed. Political organization in the state recognized the orders, though they were slightly differently arranged in different countries.

But there are some important differences, too, within the states. Perhaps these might best be characterized by a remark by the French historian Roland Mousnier.

> The kingdom of France and the land and lordships under the suzerainty of the king of France, were societies of corporations, colleges, companies, and communities – terms that were all equivalent to each other. (Mousnier, 1979, p.429)

Mousnier characterizes French society as a society of corporations, citing as examples of corporations the *parlements*, universities, craft guilds, village and parish communities, town corporations, provincial estates and assemblies.

England and Wales, Scotland and Ireland were not, by comparison, organized corporately. There were corporations – parliaments, town corporations, universities, craft guilds – but the day-to-day administration of the state did not depend upon them as it did in France. The people who ran the local administration in England and Wales – parish officers, JPs, lord lieutenants, sheriffs – did so as individuals not as members of corporations.

In Ireland one might argue that corporations were more significant. English settlers used them and Catholics were, to a large extent excluded from them, though there were Catholic Old English members of town corporations and even of parliament until surprisingly late in the seventeenth century. English society in Ireland might be described as more corporately organized than England because there was probably a greater perception of groups with common interests which needed defending. In Scotland probably the most important corporation was the church. The attempt to impose a system of JPs had not been successful and the organization of localities relied on the parish (which as in England had civil as well as ecclesiastical functions), on the ancient hierarchy of lords and tenants, and on the burghs.

It is tempting on this basis to characterize France as a society of corporations and England as a society of individuals and Scotland and

Ireland somewhere between, but we should resist this as an over-simplification. Let us return to Offprint 1 on the peculiarities of the English state, not so much to identify the peculiarities of England, as for the article's comparative perspective.

You will have appreciated that in your first reading of the article you were concentrating on definitions which had been drawn from other people's writings which we could perfectly well have taken from those writings themselves. However, we now turn to the reason why we chose this piece. Aylmer is a much-respected seventeenth-century historian who is best known for his work on the civil services of Charles I and the Commonwealth. It is for his ability to see definitions of the state in the light of seventeenth-century developments that I have chosen the article. It originally contained more comparative material, especially with states outside Europe, which has been omitted in the interests of saving space. Now read pp.6–12 of the article.

Though Aylmer does not discuss corporations, the examples he gives of English, Scottish and Irish state institutions all stress the role of individuals, with the exception of parliament. He makes the important point, too, that the English judicial system marked 'the legal supremacy of the central state, but not a centralized system of judicial administration'.

Exercise   What comparisons does Aylmer make between the English and French states?

Discussion   A number of the points will be familiar to you from discussions earlier in the unit. Let me list the main points I found:

1   equivalence of the royal households;

2   much smaller numbers of office-holders in England both at the centre and in the provinces than in France;

3   lack of a local bureaucracy in England, instead dependence on part-time and semi-amateur local administrators whereas France had a large professional bureaucracy;

4   the importance of the gentry in the lower house of parliament;

5   the absence of private jurisdictions in England;

6   the lack of semi-independent regions or provinces within the kingdom.

Most of these points apply to Scotland and Ireland. The king maintained residences in Scotland and had household officers there; in Ireland the lord or deputy lieutenant had a small court of his own at Dublin Castle. Neither country had many office-holders; Aylmer makes the point that Scotland was a less governed country than England and the same might be said of Ireland. Neither country had much in the way of local administration, though in both, borough or burgh corporations were powerful.

It is not clear that there was any group in Scotland or Ireland equivalent to the English gentry. In both countries there were regions where local nobles were more influential than the monarch, especially the more distant parts of the Scottish Highlands and Connaught in

Ireland, though their powers were being eroded in the early seventeenth century.

Aylmer raises the issue of whether Scotland, Ireland and Wales were semi-independent entities within the kingdom, but if we adopt the idea of the British Isles as a multiple kingdom, we can say that each nation had a king (or, Wales, a prince) and within each nation there were no semi-independent regions and within kingdoms and the principality the king's authority was the same everywhere.

The material world of the rural population

So far we have been concentrating on documentary evidence. I want to conclude this unit by considering a different kind of evidence for how people lived: their houses. Little remains of the buildings of the very poorest except for archaeological evidence because many people lived in rudimentary structures made from local materials.

Few of the poorest people's buildings even boasted a proper timber frame, certainly they had nothing like the jointed timber frames of buildings you see today in many areas of France and the British Isles. They were made from any materials at hand: stone, sticks or mud; bricks made from unbaked clay from the surrounding area; turf; or rubble. Roofs were usually some kind of thatch. Reeds and straw were the best materials but other materials such as heather, or broom (you can see a roof thatched with broom in TV3) were used. Most of these structures were simply a single room with a centrally placed hearth and sometimes a hole in the roof to let the smoke out. English visitors complained bitterly that Irish cabins, as they were known, had no hole in the roof and were filled with smoke.

Figure 1.
An Irish cabin, from
Mullagh, detail from a map
by Thomas Raven.
Reproduced by permission of
the North Down Heritage
Centre, Bangor.

Such buildings have not survived for two reasons. The first is that they were made from insubstantial materials. The second is that the histories of the various countries have militated against their survival and, in the cases of Ireland and Scotland, against the survival of rural houses of the more prosperous tenantry. In Ireland the displacement of the native Irish population in the later seventeenth century led to the destruction of many of their houses. Where they were permitted to remain in areas settled by the English and Scots, they were generally neither allowed nor able to afford to build anything other than the simplest and most impermanent dwellings. Simple rural Scottish dwellings did not survive the Highland clearances of the nineteenth century. In England and France greater prosperity meant the replacement of older dwellings by more permanent structures.

However, buildings erected as houses for people of slightly higher social and economic status survive in great numbers. Such people were often simply farmers, though they might have pretensions to gentle or noble status. Their houses were, like those of poorer people, built from local materials adapted to local circumstances. Like the most humble dwellings they are known as vernacular buildings as opposed to buildings that were designed according to the canons of metropolitan taste. Vernacular buildings use local forms, local materials and are adapted to local requirements.

We shall look at four gentry buildings from Wales in detail because there is a wealth of information to be gathered from them about how people lived, but buildings do not always yield up that information quite as readily as printed texts. So you will start with an exercise on how to 'read' a building. We have given you a Welsh example, but the tech-

Figure 2
An old house near Strata Florida, Cardiganshire, as recorded in 1888. Drawing reproduced by permission of the Cambrian Archaeological Association, from Peter Smith, Houses of the Welsh Countryside, *1975, HMSO.*

niques of analysis you will learn may be applied to any such simple building, whether an English long house, a Breton farm, or a house in the
Midi.

Now work on Video 1. Watch Part 1 of the video, you will be told when to
stop the tape and do Exercise 1. You will need the Illustration Book for
this exercise.

Video Exercise 1 1   Go through Part 1 of the video again listing the questions we have
                         asked about the house.

                    2   See how many of the questions you can answer, however tentatively,
                         writing down what kinds of sources you might need to consult for
                         additional information.

                    3   Referring to the plan of Llannerch-y-cawr (Pl.2) note what changes
                         appear to have taken place since it was built and say what these
                         changes can tell us about how the house's functions altered in the
                         seventeenth century.

Discussion   Now play Part 2 for the discussion of these questions.
                When you have done that, watch Part 3; you will be told when to
                stop the tape and do Exercise 2.

Video Exercise 2   Old Rhydycarw shows what Llannerch-y-cawr was originally, before being
                adapted. Plasauduon shows what someone building a new house rather
                than adapting an old one would erect. Compare Plasauduon with
                Llannerch-y-cawr, making notes on their common features and their
                differences.

Discussion   As similar features I noted that both were working farms with gentry
                pretensions and that both had a central chimney with the staircase next
                to it.
                     As differences I noted that Plasauduon was aligned *along* the
                contour, there was no question of needing to be uphill from the animals.
                The building is symmetrical with a concern for appearance, both in the
                decoration and the structure, as a display of the builder's wealth. At
                Llannerch-y-cawr a modest building was improved; at Plasauduon features
                from much grander buildings (the porch and the jettied (overhanging)
                first floor, for example) are adapted to one of a more modest scale.
                     Inside there is more private space at Plasauduon, space which
                people do not have to walk through to get from one part of the building
                to another, and there is a greater differentiation in the use of space. The
                parlour has a grand overmantel and cooking takes place in a separate
                kitchen at the back of the building.
                     Now view part 4 of the tape and when you reach the end, do
                Exercise 3.

Video Exercise 3   Having now looked at four vernacular buildings, let us consider what a historian can learn from such detailed studies.

1   What may we learn from the study of vernacular buildings and what limitations are there to what we may learn from the buildings alone?

2   What have we learned about living standards and how did we do this?

Discussion   1   Although the builders of these Welsh houses were gentry and left wills, there is rarely much in the written record about the lives of such people. By looking at their houses, we are placing people very clearly in a particular regional setting. We can see how their livelihoods structured their living accommodation and how domestic arrangements changed over the period.

Figure 3
An outline map of Wales showing the location of the four houses featured in Video 1.

But you will have noticed that each building at which we looked only provided a partial answer to our questions about construction and living standards. We needed the evidence culled from written records (Mr Brooksby referred to wills and inventories); we needed technical evidence from dendrochronology (the dating of timber from tree rings) and knowledge of techniques of building a timber frame. We also used comparison between buildings in the same area to build up a cumulative picture of change over the period. Each building on its own is part of a jigsaw.

2   We learned that living standards improved, that people increasingly divided up the space within their houses to give themselves more comfort and privacy, separating themselves both from the animals of the farm and their servants.

The way in which we actually deduced this was by looking at the placing of the chimney. At Old Rhydycarw there was only a central hearth, there was some unheated space at the end of the building behind the screen, but everyone lived for most of the time in a common space. At Llannerch-y-cawr the common space was divided up by the insertion of a chimney and a staircase, providing two rooms on the ground floor and new living space on the first floor. However, this space wasn't very convenient, those rooms which could not be reached from the stair or the entrance could only be reached through other rooms. At Plasauduon the central chimney and staircase provide better circulation, partly because the house was built all at the same period, but the chimney stack still prevented access to all rooms from a hall or corridor. It is only with the combination of a central stair and chimneys at the ends of the building that it is possible to devise a system where all the rooms could be reached from a public space, but notice how that space has diminished in relative size from a public space for the whole household to a modest entrance hall. The central stair also allows the kitchen to be placed in the basement.

References

Aylmer, G.E. (1974), *The King's Servants: The Civil Service of Charles I 1625–42*, revised edition, Routledge and Kegan Paul, London.

Bercé, Y-M. (1990), *History of Peasant Revolts*, Polity, London.

Bonney, R. (1988), *Society and Government in France under Richelieu and Mazarin 1624–61*, Macmillan, London.

Dures, A. (1983), *English Catholicism 1558–1642*, Longman, London.

Gardiner, S.R. (1906), *Constitutional Documents of the Puritan Revolution 1625–1660*, 3rd edn, Oxford University Press, Oxford.

Hughes, A. (1980), *Seventeenth-Century England: A Changing Culture, volume 1: Primary Sources*, Ward Lock, London.

Kelly, J. (1984), *Women, History and Theory*, University of Chicago Press, Chicago.

Marwick, A. (1990), *The Nature of History*, 3rd edn, Macmillan, London.

Moody, T.W., Martin, F.X. and Byrne, F.J. (1978), *A New History of Ireland, vol. III Early Modern Ireland 1534–1691*, revised edn, Oxford University Press, Oxford.

Mousnier, R. (1979), *The Institutions of France under the Absolute Monarchy 1598–1789*, University of Chicago Press, Chicago. (French edn, 1974.)

Slack, P. (1988), *Poverty and Policy in Tudor and Stuart England*, Longman, London.

Thirsk, J. and Cooper, J.P. (1972), *Seventeenth Century Economic Documents*, Clarendon Press, Oxford.

Unit 2
Apprentices in absolutism

*Prepared for the course team by
Lucille Kekewich*

Contents

Study timetable

Weeks of study	Texts	Video	AC	Set books
2	Unit 2; *Anthology* I.5,6,7,8,9,10, 11; Offprints 2,3; Illustration Book	Video 2		Coward, Briggs

During the period of this unit you will also need to watch TV3 and 4.

Objectives

The objectives of this unit are to help you to:

1   understand the élite political culture and the ways in which it might contribute to an increase in royal power;

2   discern elements in the workings of the courts which could contribute to the exercise of royal power or the breakdown of royal authority;

3   understand some of the reasons for the relative success or failure of the French and British state fiscal systems and methods of enforcing obedience.

Introduction

The first part of this unit will be devoted to a study of the British and French courts and of how Charles I and Louis XIII used courtiers in their government. The importance attached to this subject is in itself a sign of changing historical thought. A few decades ago Sir Geoffrey Elton postulated a Tudor revolution in government which moved power away from the royal household to the council and its ministers. However, David Starkey (1987) took issue with Elton's approach claiming that the courtiers who were in regular contact with the monarch continued to be of considerable political importance into the reign of Charles I, as were the personalities of the king and those who served him. There was no realistic way in which the public function of the monarchy in conducting the government of the realm could be separated from its private life in the court. We will test this hypothesis, and its application to France as well as to the British Isles.

What exactly was the court and how can it be distinguished from the royal households? The court in England or France was the sum of all those who regularly gathered round the king at his residence who had legitimate business to be there. It was a locus of influence where favour and patronage could make a difference to peoples' lives and to the course of government.

Figure 4 Charles I *by Gerard Honthorst, 1628, oil on canvas 76.2 x 64.1cm. National Portrait Gallery, London.*

Figure 5 Louis XIII around the age of 21 *by Peter Paul Rubens, c.1622–5, oil on canvas, 118.11 x 96.52 cm. The Norton Simon Foundation, Pasadena, California F.1965.1.60.P.*

The lavish display encouraged by the French and British monarchies was indicative of real power, not just a propaganda facade.

The most stable elements within the court were the royal households. The kings had the largest: hundreds of men and a few women from the greatest officers, chamberlains and masters of the horse, to pastry cooks and seamstresses. Their queens had separate households, more female in character but reflecting, on a smaller scale, the hierarchical structure which served their husbands. Louis XIII had to contend with the households of his mother, Marie de Medici, and brother, Gaston of Orléans, whose subversive activities gave both the status of rival courts. This was an element in the political troubles which ensued.

The presence of the monarch determined the existence of a court, therefore when Louis went hunting at Versailles or campaigning in the south a scaled-down court accompanied him. However, Charles I's court rarely moved beyond his houses and palaces in and around London and noble houses in the home counties, with the exception of his visit to Scotland for his coronation in 1633. This restricted, to a limited area, the glamour and potential for propaganda which came with the royal court and this would have serious implications for the king later in his reign.

Exercise   Read the two letters written by James Howell from Edinburgh and Dublin (*Anthology*, I.5), look at the map of the campaigns of Louis XIII in France (Col.Pl.4) and read Briggs, pp.84–105.
How important was the presence of a king and court to the effective execution of Royal policies?

Discussion   Howell found a very depressing situation in Edinburgh. Despite the quality of the city and his reference to Holyrood Palace, there was an authority vacuum. Lord Traquair, a mere royal commissioner, had been unable to implement the king's religious policy: 'The Bishops are all gone to wreck'. The writer put his finger on one cause of the problem,

Figure 6
Peter Paul Rubens, St George and the Dragon, *1629–30, oil on canvas, 153 x 226 cm. The Royal Collection © 1994 Her Majesty the Queen.*

the king had not sat with parliament in its new building: 'they did ill who advised him ...'

As Thomas Wentworth exercised royal power and prerogatives as Lord Deputy of Ireland, Howell correctly described his presence at Dublin Castle as a 'court'. He proceeded to make suit to Wentworth for the place of the languishing Sir William Usher as Clerk of the Council, and was given an encouraging answer. This was exactly how monarchs could use the vast court patronage at their disposal to confirm the loyalty of key supporters and to extend their power.

Briggs in the extract you have just read tends to attribute the formulation of internal and foreign policies to Richelieu, Louis XIII's chief minister from 1624, rather than to the king. Yet the map of the movements of Louis, 1614–42, shows an energetic monarch taking initiatives well before Richelieu's time. Briggs demonstrates that most of the king's campaigns, both against his own subjects and his foreign enemies, were successful. There could well have been a connection between this and the fact that he and his court were frequently moving about France. Louis dispensed favours and punishments on his progresses and his following spent considerable sums of money. Provincial governors and magnates knew that they might have to answer directly to their royal master and ordinary people saw their king in all his glory pass by.

Both monarchs recognized the importance of maintaining a splendid palace as a setting for the court in their capital cities. Whitehall, adjacent to Westminster Abbey and the Thames, was the principal residence of Charles I. He could also conveniently visit Windsor Castle, Greenwich and Hampton Court palaces and houses such as Theobalds in Hertfordshire. Louis XIII, a keen huntsman like Charles I, frequently visited his childhood home of St Germain-en-Laye, Fontainebleau and the lodge at Versailles. His most important palace, however, was the Louvre, by the river Seine in Paris (see TV1). Now turn to Video 2 for an exercise which will introduce you to the appearance and layout of the palaces of Whitehall and the Louvre.

Exercise Read Batiffol (Offprint 3, pp.21–4) and Sharpe (Offprint 2, p.17), as well as *Anthology*, I.6.

1   What kind of political advantages could monarchs derive from the ceremonies described?

2   Was there any difference in style between the English and French ceremonies?

Discussion 1   The reception of ambassadors was of great importance in defining relationships with foreign powers. When the crown wished to establish or enhance alliances, costs incurred in honouring the country through its ambassadors were worthwhile. The marriage of Henrietta Maria to Charles I was an important factor in the diplomatic volte-face in which Britain decided that friendship with France was preferable to an alliance with the Habsburgs: the union had to be concluded with the maximum of lavish ceremonial

Figure 7
After Sir Anthony Van Dyck,
Henrietta Maria, c.*1632–5,*
oil on canvas, 109.2x82.6 cm.
National Portrait Gallery,
London.

on both sides of the Channel. The St George's Day procession gave evidence of the links existing in the mind of Charles I between religion, the monarchy and English traditions. This led him to make an uncharacteristically public display of his commitment to the ideals embodied in the Order of the Garter.

2   The nature of the evidence to be found in the accounts differs considerably: Sharpe and Batiffol are based on compilations from original sources, Chamberlain was a contemporary witness. The latter was highly coloured and critical, the informality of the tone showed the gap between the theories which informed the ceremonies and the way in which they were received by ordinary subjects. If we had an equivalent French account would it have been any more respectful? Apart from the francophobia which pervaded Chamberlain's account, there was a feeling that the French were more accustomed to lavish displays. The banquets had 'not been seen in these parts …' 'wherein we came no near them …' Both courts seem to have placed a high value on dignity, magnificence and precedence.

Both kings were reacting against the relative informality of their fathers' courts in wishing to establish a very carefully defined ceremonial code. The main difference between them that comes out in these extracts is that the Louvre events were only witnessed by courtiers and foreign plenipotentiaries. Henrietta Maria's reception in England was rather more in the public domain and the St George's Day festivities were deliberately given a popular dimension. Yet we know that this conclusion could be misleading, Charles was only visible to a limited number of his subjects whilst every year Louis XIII travelled widely throughout France and spent time with his soldiers in their camps.

Figure 8
Gerrit Houckgeest, Charles
I, Henrietta Maria dining
in public, *1635, oil on*
panel, 63.2 x 92.4 cm. The
Royal Collection © 1994 Her
Majesty the Queen.

Politics and the court

So far we have considered some evidence to support Starkey's claim that the government of the realms was intimately associated with the organization and the personnel of the royal courts. There are further questions, however, to be answered: what categories of people became courtiers?; how did they ingratiate themselves with the monarchs, their families, favourites and ministers?; how did they finance the considerable cost of being a courtier?

You will have some idea of the answer to the first question from your readings in Batiffol and Sharpe. In both countries the high nobility occupied the major positions at court; the lesser tended to go to gentlemen in England, to minor nobles in France. The common people carried out the host of menial tasks required for the smooth operation of both courts. The services of professionals such as doctors, scholars and lawyers were also needed, and many of those who possessed those skills were drawn from the middle classes or bourgeoisie. Powerful women also had their place: governesses of the young princes could be influential and were drawn from the higher nobility. Many of the major offices in the queens' households were held by great noblewomen.

Religion was an essential element in the culture of each court; both kings were pious and regularly attended services. In France only Catholic bishops, priests and religious were allowed to function in the court. From 1625 in England a strong contingent of Anglicans had, grudgingly, to make room for the few Catholic priests who, by treaty, were to minister to Henrietta Maria. Inigo Jones built her a chapel which still exists, a decent distance from Whitehall Palace, near St James's Palace.

James Howell's letter from Dublin (*Anthology*, I.5(B)) demonstrated the process by which prospective courtiers might acquire posts. Once a man, or a woman, had gained an office they could utilize their new standing to make contacts and display their wit, industry, beauty or whatever assets they might possess, to gain further advancement. Only the greatest nobles could rely on their birth to give them automatic precedence at court. The Duke of Chevreuse, a member of the powerful Guise family, was a suitable proxy for Charles I at the betrothal ceremony at the Louvre. The Duke of Buckingham, however, was an exception. The son of an obscure country gentleman, he had, by 1625, a position so commanding that he could entertain the French embassy in a state which replicated the royal hospitality (see *Anthology*, I.6). Favourites, utterly dependent on the king, could be an effective means of implementing his will; they could also cause disfunction in the court:

> ... the ruler could disturb the settled expectations of his court ... by the elevation of a favourite. (Evans, 1991, p.486)

So powerful were ministers and favourites like Buckingham, Strafford, de Luynes and Richelieu that they had patronage networks that were, to some extent, separate from royal grants of favour. Yet all ultimately derived from the monarch; power and clients could disappear overnight as Strafford discovered in 1641.

Figure 9
Queens Chapel, St James's, London. Drawing reproduced from Open London, *1988, Open University.*

Figure 10
Peter Paul Rubens, George Villiers, Duke of Buckingham, *1625, black, red and white chalk on paper with brush and ink on the eyes, 38.3 x 26.3 cm. Graphische Sammlung Albertina, Vienna.*

Exercise   Read Coward, pp.147–50 and 152–8 and refer again to Briggs, pp. 83–8.

1   Compare the rise of the Duke de Luynes and the Duke of Buckingham.

2   How could you distinguish a royal favourite from a royal minister?

Discussion 1   De Luynes, like Buckingham, was handsome and athletic, a man of the world who was probably perceived by the young Louis as some sort of father figure. He took the lead in destroying Concini, the favourite of the Queen Mother, so his rise to power was confirmed by a political act pleasing to the king. No such circumstances attended Buckingham's ascent: a charming manner and his homoerotic qualities recommended him to James. The favourites both exploited their positions to build up a <u>large following of clients,</u> gain good posts and marriages for their families and huge private wealth. De Luynes died unexpectedly at the end of 1621 and was replaced a few years later by Richelieu who was a chief minister rather than a favourite. Buckingham allowed able ministers such as Lionel Cranfield and Francis Bacon to be disgraced. After Buckingham's murder in 1628 Charles had no more favourites.

2   The difference between favourites and ministers is hard to define. The affections of a monarch were engaged in the career of a favourite and he or she would enjoy a degree of personal contact and protection not extended to even the most useful minister. Some favourites were able but, in the case of de Luynes and Buckingham, if either had been physically unattractive their mediocre talents as soldiers and politicians would have been unlikely to have gained them advancement.

Exercise   Refer to Briggs, pp.89–90 and *Anthology*, I.7 for the accounts they give of how Richelieu established a strong, long-standing influence over Louis XIII and of Strafford as Lord Deputy in Ireland. How secure was the position of each of these two royal servants?

Discussion Not at all secure! Richelieu, according to Briggs, had to work hard to persuade Louis XIII to adopt a chosen policy. The king's withdrawn and suspicious character made him difficult to lead. The cardinal had the advantages of noble birth, high ecclesiastical rank and great ability. Without the dedicated tact which he exercised for twenty years, however, it is unlikely that he would have survived in favour (you will read below about two French nobles who did not).

Strafford's tone throughout the letter was defensive although he was writing to a friend and confidante. He lacked the high birth, independent status and regular close contact with Charles I which provided such advantages to Richelieu. In Ireland, however, he was extremely powerful with his great residences, huge private income and troop of a hundred horse. His problem was that the means by which he achieved his power and his implementation of royal policies made him extremely unpopular in England as well as in Ireland.

The rewards for a successful courtier were prominence, power (or at least influence) and 'perks'. The direct and indirect financial returns for service at court were strong incentives for the impecunious younger sons of the nobility and gentry, owners of unprofitable estates and the basely born. Yet the French and British monarchs experienced considerable difficulty in giving sufficient financial rewards to their courtiers. They suffered as much as their subjects from the effects of the declining value of land rents. Huge sums of money were required to keep themselves and their expanding families in appropriate royal state. Warfare cost more than ever and, although it was possible to raise extra money in taxation, this led to bruising confrontations and rebellions. Both kings had a large number of posts in their gift, ranging from the great offices of state and in the households to positions as wolf-hunters (France) and park-keepers (Britain). They also could reward good service by grants of land or pensions. There was, however, a divergence between the two kingdoms in some of the methods by which favours were distributed:

> The sale of offices by the crown, not by office-holders themselves, was an exception in England, but undoubtedly the grant of monopolies was in many ways comparable to the trade in offices that was widely practised in early modern France and other continental European countries. (Asch, 1991, p.359)

Yet neither the selling of offices in France nor the granting of monopolies in the British Isles were neutral acts. The possession of the resources and influence to acquire an office was no guarantee of the qualifications required to do the work effectively (some offices were, of course, sinecures). Tenure of many offices in France gave exemption from certain taxes, this caused resentment on the part of the majority who had no offices and resulted in the impoverishment of the crown. Another problem was that many of those who had purchased offices were disappointed that the profits they yielded fell short of their expectations. In this way a device which should have confirmed the loyalty of many influential people to the crown instead alienated them from it. (See Briggs, pp.96–7 and Appendix graph 7.) Monopolies were generally detested in the British Isles: workers in trades where whole or partial ones existed were harmed or even ruined. The people at large saw monopolies as a means of allowing undeserving courtiers to sell inferior goods and services at artificially high prices.

In the middle years of the century Charles I and the French regent, Anne of Austria, were to feel the impact of the alienation of large bodies of their subjects from the crown. The way in which the royal courts had been financed over the previous decades was to be one of the major grievances voiced in Britain and in France.

Figure 11
Anne of Austria in her mid 20s *by Peter Paul Rubens, c.1622–5, oil on canvas, 120.65 x 96.84 cm. The Norton Simon Foundation, Pasadena, California F.1965.1.59.P.*

The imagery of monarchy

The introduction to this unit has shown how important it was for the monarchs to maintain a suitably magnificent and elevated estate. Block 3, Unit 13 will discuss the scriptural basis for the idea that kings ruled by 'divine right' and how this could be a justification for absolutist rule. Any king who wished his subjects to endow him with god-like qualities had to live up to the role in both his appearance and behaviour. Sir Philip Warwick wrote of Charles I:

> His deportment was very majestic; for he would not let fall his dignity, no not to the greatest foreigners that came to visit him and his court; for though he was far from pride, yet he was careful of majesty, and would be approached with respect and reverence. (Ollard, 1979, p.28)

In a letter to his old governess Louis XIII wrote:

> For piety St Louis
> For clemency Henri IV
> For justice Louis XII
> For love of truth Pharamont [a Frankish chief, often called first king of France]
> For valour Charlemagne
> And for temperance Charles V
> And Louis XIII will surpass all these kings by the grace of God.
>
> (Moote, 1989, p.37)

Exercise Look at the portraits of Charles I and Louis XIII (Illustration Book plates 9 and 10).

1   Contrast the style and artistic programmes of the two pictures.

2   In what ways were they likely to enhance the image of monarchy?

Discussion 1   There is an important difference in the scale and medium of the two pictures. The van Dyck is an oil painting, showing Charles I indulging in the kingly sport of hunting, the impact it makes on the observer is more direct than that of the impersonal bust of Louis XIII which is a small portrait at the front of a book. The most obvious contrast between the portraits is the humanity and informality of Charles I in comparison with the classical severity of Louis XIII. Little distinguishes the costume of the English king from that of an ordinary country gentleman. The setting in an open landscape heightens the impression.

De Lasne's portrait of Louis could be carved in stone, remote and terrible. Much of the page was devoted to reinforcing the impact using classical imagery and reminders of the victories of the warrior-king. Yet his face was not idealized, his nose is shown to be prominent and there are bags under his eyes. Charles I, on the other hand (we know from written accounts), was slight of stature with bandy legs. The artistry of van Dyck concealed these unkingly attributes and, in a more subtle fashion than de Lasne, conveyed the image of a powerful king.

2   The apparently nonchalant attitude of Charles conveys great authority. The steady gaze with which he engages the viewer is not the
kind of look given to an equal. The horse looks submissive and the
two subordinate figures, both rendering services, enhance the king's
superiority. The size of the painting (272 x 212 cm.) would further
increase its impact.

Louis XIII wears the laurel wreath and armour of a Roman
emperor, the portrait is supported on either side by a classical deity
(Mars and Minerva: war and wisdom). Four oval pictures recall
some of his military victories. As the frontispiece of a book which
contained a justification of the king's rights to unlimited power, it
would have been distributed fairly widely in literate circles.

A monarch's building policy could affirm, as emphatically as his portraits,
his aspirations to enjoy unlimited authority. Paradoxically the two most
spectacular palaces built in the earlier part of the century were commissioned by queens. The new palace at Greenwich was started by Inigo
Jones for Anne of Denmark and enjoyed by Henrietta Maria. The Lux-
embourg in Paris was built for Marie de Medici, it incorporated many of
the features of her childhood home in the Pitti Palace, in Florence, and
was a source of Italian influence on French art (see TV1).

Both Louis and Charles were prepared to continue the grand building projects they had inherited from their mothers. An important part of
the prestige of their palaces, houses, castles and lodges was that they
should be well furnished and filled with all manner of valuable objects.
The kings inherited a great array of precious possessions and they were
both collectors. They also commissioned a number of portraits and other
paintings. Neither country had a flourishing native school so both
employed Flemish painters such as Rubens and Dutchmen like Pourbus
and Mytens. In England there was a taste for Italian art, at least at court.
Critics of Charles I and his queen feared that popish doctrines would be
smuggled in with the Raphaels and Bellinis. The papacy certainly bom-
barded the king with art works hoping, presumably, to achieve that result.

Exercise   Read Batiffol (Offprint 3, pp.19–21) and *Anthology*, I.8.

1   What contrasts emerge between the taste of the two kings?

2   Would the nature of their collections have affected the way in which
they were perceived?

Discussion 1   The nature of the evidence used for the collections differs: Batiffol
drew on primary sources to compile an overview of all the
collections of Henri IV and Louis XIII. Abraham van der Doort was
a contemporary who conscientiously catalogued all the pictures in
his charge (he also listed sculpture, coins and other precious
objects) and we have only seen an extract. It is clear that Louis and
Charles had different approaches to their collections. The
Bourbons had inherited a rich hoard of goods from earlier royal
dynasties and regarded them with veneration: signing their names
in the bible of Charles V (the Wise). The expansive Henri liked to

show off his treasures, Louis preferred to resort alone to his cabinet for pleasure, mostly of a practical kind: painting, designing, composing music and printing.

Charles had been collecting since his youth and had an approach closer to that of a modern connoisseur and he was single-minded in his pursuit of attractive newer paintings. The king had considerable knowledge and excellent taste, most of the pictures mentioned in the extract had been painted in the previous hundred years. Foreign visitors knew that prestigious Masters would be very acceptable gifts; the king's ambassadors and servants searched the continental market for acquisitions.

2   The attitude of both monarchs to their collections had political consequences. In the early seventeenth century the Bourbons were still a rather new dynasty and Henri IV was probably quite consciously establishing links with a revered medieval king such as Charles V. (A picture of Louis XIII presenting the church of St Paul and St Louis en Marais to his namesake, St Louis, made the same point.) The collections of armour, birds and beasts were traditional in royal households (Charles had them as well) and contributed to the spectacular quality of the court. Louis was an enthusiastic soldier and his keen interest in arms and other martial matters paid large dividends in his military successes.

The European reputation that Charles enjoyed as an art collector enhanced his prestige with other monarchs and amongst scholars and artists. His English subjects, however, were likely to estimate the value of a picture, not by its aesthetic qualities, but by the way in which it displayed the importance of the owner. Old Tudor portraits could do this just as well as expensive paintings by Titian. The perceived extravagance of Charles's court and the way in which he financed it proved to be a grievance for a substantial number of his subjects. This was exacerbated by his love of Italian works which were thought to be infected with Catholicism.

Writers could make an important contribution to the way in which the king was perceived, especially by his literate subjects. (See Unit 6 for a discussion of popular literacy.) Louis XIII and Charles I provided plenty of evidence that they appreciated the political importance of literature and knew how to extend or withhold their patronage. The products of good Renaissance educations, they had a proper respect for the conventions of classical decorum in literature as well as in art. They also expected their writers to support and praise their policies and their persons. Abraham Cowley, whilst still a teenager, applauded Charles's visit to Scotland in 1633:

> Welcome, great Sir, with all the joy that's due
> To the return of Peace and you.
> Two greatest blessings which this age can know;
> For that to thee, for thee to heaven we owe.
> Others by war their conquests gain.
> You like a god your ends obtain,
> Who when rude chaos for his help did call
> Spoke but the word, and sweetly ordered all.

(Pickel, 1936, p. 59)

Louis too received numerous laudatory poems and, with Richelieu, also encouraged prose works which would justify and applaud their policies. Professional writers such as Guez de Balzac and Nicolas Faret emphasized the special wisdom which enabled the king and his ministers to rule justly and the need for strong government control to curb disorder in the state.

Exercise   Re-read Cowley's poem and the extract from Faret (*Anthology*, I.9).
How do the two writers interpret their role in these extracts?

Discussion   The occasions for these pieces were different: Cowley's poem was directly addressed to Charles. Faret was writing in the context of the court but he intended his audience to be other courtiers rather than the king. Cowley treated Charles with slavish adulation, supporting the policy of ensuring tranquillity in his Northern kingdom by a visit and, optimistically, predicting an entirely successful outcome. Faret described the monarch in suitably obsequious terms: 'this great light' and imputed any problems which might arise to those around him. His advice was, nevertheless, grimly practical, the dangers inherent in a self-seeking and strife-torn court could threaten the stability of the state. It is arguable that Faret chose to render a more useful service to Louis, by the realistic advice he offered to his courtiers, than Cowley who was simply regurgitating for Charles the king's own most sanguine views of his policies and capacities.

Faret described the court as a 'theatre'; the kings, both theatre lovers, and their followers in England and in France, seem to have played their parts quite consciously and deliberately. Illusion and reality could, at times, be almost indistinguishable. Charles and Louis were prepared to fund and participate in masques and 'ballets de cour' (court ballets). With their idealized plots and gorgeous clothes and scenery these were the closest the monarchs could get to the harmony between state and subjects which their exercise of unlimited power was supposed to prod- uce. Turn now to Video 2.

The nobility in court and country

Amongst the artists, professional men, lowly born servants, priests and other categories of people who made up the royal courts in the British Isles and France, the great nobles enjoyed a unique position. Unless specifically forbidden the king's presence, their high birth and the wealth and influence these gave them, carried with it an automatic right to prominence at court. Others achieved the same result by becoming royal favourites or by outstanding service. Not all great nobles wished to exercise their privileges: some preferred to remain on their provincial estates, enjoying power based on their locality; others shunned the expense of court life or disapproved of its prevailing political or moral tone. In this section we will look briefly at the careers of three nobles bearing the following questions in mind. What relationship was there between favour at court and a successful career as a magnate? Did these nobles assist or impede the attempts of Charles I and Louis XIII to exercise unlimited power in their realms?

The Duke of Épernon

Figure 12
Jean-Louis de Nogaret de la Valette, Duke of Épernon, *medal designed by Guillaume Dupré. Bibliothèque Nationale, Cabinet des Médailles, Paris.*

Jean Louis de Nogaret, Duke of Épernon (1554–1642) began his career as a minor noble at Loches in Languedoc, an area remote from Paris which prized its regional customs and privileges. He rose rapidly in favour at the court of Henri III to whom he gave effective military support throughout the fluctuating alliances of the Wars of Religion. By the 1580s, together with the Duke of Joyeuse, he was a principal royal favourite. His marriage to the heiress Marguerite de Foix and de Candalle brought him great wealth and standing in Gascony. When Henri IV succeeded on the assassination of Henri III he retained his power but lost the intimacy with the king he had formerly enjoyed as a royal favourite.

Épernon continued to receive honours and high offices and Henri IV encouraged him to spend lavishly on a large new château at Cadillac, just outside Bordeaux. During the next few decades it was decorated by artists such as Pierre Souffron, Jean Langlois and the Pageot and Coutereau families. It was filled with costly furniture including a number of tapestries which had been specially commissioned. Épernon still spent much time at court and was riding with Henri IV in his coach when the king was assassinated.

Épernon had three sons: the eldest became a Protestant for a time, differed with his strongly orthodox and irascible father and spent most of his life on military campaigns abroad. The second son, Bernard was also a soldier and was made Duke de la Valette in 1622. He married an illegitimate daughter of Henri IV, a considerable honour as she ranked as a foreign princess in the court's order of precedence. His youngest son gained rapid preferment in the church and eventually became Cardinal de la Valette.

In 1622 Épernon was given the prestigious governorship of Guyenne (a huge area in south-west France) and took up residence in the castle at Bordeaux. During the sixteen years that he held the post, the state gradually eroded the powers of provincial governors by the appointment of *intendants*. These were usually men of lower social position than the governors and they were directly dependent on the crown (see Briggs, pp.119–20). For the rest of Épernon's life he made very few visits to the royal court. The rapid rise of his family through three reigns had made him a mighty territorial magnate and according to Fessenden (1972) he enjoyed an income of about 300,000 livres per annum. He spent lavishly and anyone who opposed his will in Guyenne was likely to be insulted or beaten up as he had formidable resources of manpower and patronage:

> … [he] used his clients to dominate the municipal government of Bordeaux. The city was divided into six districts, or *jurades*, from which one *jurat* [councillor] was elected … Occasionally the governor would suspend elections and name the *jurats* himself by royal letters, as in 1627 and 1630, and there is documentary evidence that he influenced the municipal elections in 1625 and 1626 to put his own clients into office. We can infer that he manipulated elections in other years, too. … Once his clients were in office, it was easier to

Figure 13
General view of west front and stone bridge of Château de Cadillac, near Bordeaux. Photo: Lonchampt-Delehaye. Caisse National des Monuments Historiques/ DACS. London 1994.

Figure 14
Fireplace named 'Madame' in Royal Apartments, Château de Cadillac. Photo: Lonchampt-Delehaye. Caisse National des Monuments Historiques/DACS. London 1994.

Figure 15
Masque detail from fireplace in antechamber of Royal Apartments, Château de Cadillac. Photo: Lonchampt-Delehaye. Caisse National des Monuments Historiques/ DACS. London 1994.

put other clients in office ... garrison commanders included clients such as Joseph Magnas de Saint Géry, commander of Nérac, and Jean-Louis de la Valette, an illegitimate son, commander of Bergerac. The duc d'Épernon was able to muster at least 600 nobles from Guyenne for his military campaigns, and his entourage included noble clients from the region. Épernon's household numbered more than sixty servants and cost him 60,000 livres in 1639. He employed four secretaries. (Kettering, 1986, pp.74, 96)

During the early years of his governorship, Épernon was involved in a number of disputes about the limits of his authority with the *parlement* of Bordeaux, which had enjoyed considerable independence as most recent governors had been absentees. The presence of a haughty governor living in their midst changed the situation. A series of ill-natured confrontations ensued ranging from matters such as his right to levy special taxes to pay for his campaigns against the Huguenots to farcical arguments about the custody of silver trumpets, access to the fishmarket and the erection of a maypole. Louis XIII and Richelieu temporized, they needed Épernon to be strong enough to raise taxes, to persecute the Huguenots and to guard a strategic frontier area. On the other hand, they did not wish him to become too powerful: compromises were effected and the disputes with the *parlement* ceased.

In 1633 Épernon over-reached himself by quarrelling with Richelieu's friend, Henri de Sourdis, archbishop of Bordeaux. Accounts of the climax of their dispute differed, but it seems that Épernon knocked the archbishop's hat off with his stick and then poked him in the stomach. De Sourdis was delighted, he immediately excommunicated Épernon and placed Bordeaux under an interdict. Most of the citizens supported their archbishop as did Louis and Richelieu. The former wrote:

> I wish to show how I love the Church ... her interests are no less to me than my own ... I would rather be dead than have touched an ecclesiastic out of anger. (Fessenden, 1972, p.111)

Épernon was probably saved from permanent disgrace by the favour his son, the cardinal, enjoyed at court. To regain his governorship and titles in 1635, however, he had to receive a humiliating absolution from de Sourdis and allow Bernard de la Valette to marry a niece of Richelieu. (It was surprising that Richelieu wanted this as de la Valette had beaten and abused his first wife in front of the whole court and was later reputed to have poisoned her.) Restored to favour, Épernon, despite his great age, vigorously suppressed popular riots against the *taille* (see Briggs, pp.129–30) in Bordeaux in 1635.

Three years later Épernon and Bernard de la Valette were finally destroyed. The latter only half-heartedly laid siege to Fontarbie in the war against Spain (see Briggs, p.109); he wrangled with Condé, the commander-in-chief, and Archbishop de Sourdis, the admiral of the fleet. When a Spanish army raised the siege, he received all the blame for the government's humiliation. He fled to England, was put on trial for treason in France in his absence, by an infuriated king, condemned and hanged in effigy. His father was stripped of all his offices and exiled to Loches where he died in 1642 at the age of 87.

returned to France after deaths of Louis & Richelieu

Exercise   Using the information given above, references to Épernon and de la Valette in Briggs and the extracts from Girard (*Anthology*, I.10), answer the following questions:

1   What factors (a) enhanced and (b) undermined the territorial power of Épernon and his family?

2   What determined the attitude of Louis and Richelieu to Épernon?

Discussion   1(a)   Épernon, one of the favourites of Henri III, was not simply ornamental: he gave valuable military service to the crown during the Wars of Religion. His three sons (including the cardinal), were also capable military leaders. Épernon's principal power base was in Guyenne. This was an area of great importance to the crown: Bordeaux was the centre of the lucrative wine trade and so was a large potential source of revenue. The area included a number of Huguenot enclaves and also gave access to the strategically vital frontier with Spain. These factors presented opportunities but also possible pitfalls to the governor. He did his best to secure control by the maintenance of loyal garrison commanders and a military entourage of nobles and their followers; he used his right to appoint *jurats* to try to ensure that the government of Bordeaux was conducted according to his wishes. The presence of his son, the cardinal, at court was extremely helpful to the whole family.

(b)   The martial qualities which had recommended Épernon to Henri III were not appreciated by the commercially minded Bordelais who mostly supported their archbishop in the fracas of 1633. Épernon's long life involved him in a change of government policy: the systematic curtailment of the independence of regional powers, including the magnates, during the mature rule of Louis XIII. His residence in Guyenne was remote from the royal court so he could not explain or defend himself against his enemies.

2   Louis's visit to Épernon's great château at Cadillac does not, despite Girard's glowing account, seem to have been an unqualified success. He only stayed for two days, possibly ten fine rooms resplendent with cloth of gold were about five rooms too many for a subject. The visit was meant to symbolize royal forgiveness for Épernon's recent misdeeds, but despite the honours he and his sons received soon afterwards, there were always royal reservations, later shared by Richelieu. Épernon's disputes as governor with the *parlement* were irritating to the king and he used them to stress that, in the last resort, both parties had to appeal to him for a verdict. The Huguenots had not been finally subdued, so Louis could not afford seriously to undermine Épernon. The king was stronger in 1633, was genuinely scandalized by the duke's conduct and humiliated him with alacrity. The exasperation of the king and cardinal over the Fontarbie affair was terminal; even the influence of Cardinal de la Valette could not save his family on this occasion. Relentlessly the king and Cardinal Richelieu seized the opportunity to make an exemplary demonstration of the power they exercised over the greatest of magnates.

The Duchess of Chevreuse

(05-109

First read Briggs on 'Noble conspiracy and rebellion', pp.~~110–14~~.

> Madame de Chevreuse was a woman in the fullest sense, in this was her strength, and also her weakness. Her first impulse was love, or rather gallantry, and the interests of the one whom she loved became her chief aim. Here lies the solution of the prodigies of sagacity, adroitness and energy which she displayed in the vain pursuit of a chimera, which constantly receded from her grasp … (Cousin, 1859, pp.3–4)

This is a fairly typical characterization of this controversial noblewoman in the centuries which preceded the advent of feminist history. Does an account of her life and any evidence which survives of her motives sustain an alternative interpretation?

Marie-Aimée was born in 1600, a daughter of the Duke of Montbazon and a member of the great de Rohan family. It was a sign of her father's prominence at court that, at the age of seventeen, she was married to the royal favourite, the Duke de Luynes. She was immediately given one of the highest positions at court available to a woman, Superintendent of the Queen's Household. This offered a unique opportunity to gain the friendship of Anne of Austria who was also seventeen. The influence the duchess exercised over the queen was to be of considerable political importance for the next two decades.

The duchess possessed the attributes of a successful favourite: outstanding beauty, vivacity, wit and intelligence. Louis XIII was also taken with her at first but, before de Luynes's sudden death in 1621, seemed to cool towards man and wife. His coolness changed to aversion when the queen, running through a hall in the Louvre, fell and later miscarried: no live heir was born until 1638. Those who had encouraged the queen to behave so unwisely were the Duchess de Luynes and Mademoiselle de Verneuil (the illegitimate daughter of Henri IV, soon to become the unfortunate first wife of Bernard de la Valette). Louis appears to have blamed the duchess for this dynastic calamity and, from then onwards, tried to keep her from the queen's presence. Despite Anne's remonstrances, the duchess and de Verneuil were banished from court.

Early in 1622, a few months after the death of de Luynes, the duchess married Claude de Lorraine, Duke of Chevreuse, without the permission of the king. This was a good move on her part: Claude was a member of the powerful Guise family, his eldest brother ruled Lorraine, technically an independent duchy. Handsome, amiable and not very assertive, he was high in favour at court and had recently been made Grand Chamberlain. Louis XIII accepted the *fait accompli* and Marie de Chevreuse resumed her duties as Superintendent of the Queen's Household. Batiffol (Offprint 3) stressed the prominent part played by the Duke and Duchess of Chevreuse in the marriage ceremonies of Charles I and Henrietta Maria. No mention was made of the liaison the duchess was conducting with one of the English ambassadors, the Earl of Holland. She also encouraged the main plenipotentiary, the Duke of Buckingham, to make advances to Anne of Austria. Although unsubstantiated, the scandalous gossip about the alleged affair was known to the king, and his relationship with his childless wife further damaged and with it, the position of her favourite.

Figure 16
The Duchess of Chevreuse,
as Diana Chasseuse,
frontispiece of Louis Batiffol,
La Duchesse de Chevreuse.
Une vie d'aventures et
d'intrigues sous Louis XIII,
*1913, Paris. Bibliothèque
Nationale, Paris.*

Frustration at her inability to exert any influence beyond the queen's quarters may explain the involvement of the Duchess of Chevreuse in the Chalais affair in 1626. The plot was to replace Louis with his brother, Gaston of Orléans. When it was discovered Gaston, as usual, escaped with a reprimand, the Count of Chalais was executed and the duchess exiled from court. Her reception of the news, if it was accurately reported by Richelieu, provides an insight into her motivation:

> … so enraged was she that, quite beside herself with fury, she said to Bautru that, as she was treated in France, so, she would see to it, would the French be treated in England: That it was within her power to bring English armies into France, if she so wished; that people did not really know her; that they thought she was interested only in coquetry; but that she would show them some day that she was capable of other things … (Lavollée, 1925, p.111; trans. by A. Scholar)

The duchess fled to Lorraine where she gained the admiration and support of her brother-in-law, Duke Charles. He was persuaded to join an anti-French coalition of the Huguenots, supported by Charles I and Buckingham, Spain, Piedmont and Savoy. Using the good offices of the ever-faithful queen and the Duke of Chevreuse, who was still in favour at court, she was reinstated in 1631. Two years later she was exiled again; she had been conducting a liaison with the Marquis of Chateauneuf who had maintained an unauthorized correspondence with foreign powers. At her château near Tours she kept a large and open household and had no difficulty in conducting a correspondence with the queen. The duchess used this to transmit, using a complex female network involving the abbess at the Val de Grâce convent, Paris, the results of her treasonable negotiations with England and Spain, and the queen became dangerously implicated. This was known to Richelieu and the king:

> When one of the Cardinal's agents, the Abbé du Dorat, said to him on August 28, 1637, 'you must be prepared for every kind of frivolity and impertinence in that sex', he accurately defined the qualities of levity and thoughtlessness inherent in ladies who dabbled in such intrigues as this one. (Batiffol, 1913, pp.163–4)

The duchess fled to Spain, disguised as a man, and then crossed to England where she was warmly received by the king and queen. With a coterie of French exiles which included, by 1639, Marie de Medici and the Duke de la Valette she continued her intrigues to undermine Louis XIII. She moved to Brussels in the following year where she became involved in the rebellion of the Count of Soissons (see Briggs, p.109).

The deaths of Richelieu in 1642 and of Louis in the following year, removed the obstacles to the return to France of the duchess. Anne of Austria, regent for the young Louis XIV, recalled her just a month after the king died. It was six years since Anne and her former favourite had met and the queen was becoming increasingly reliant on Cardinal Mazarin. The Duchess of Chevreuse was frustrated that, possessed at last of real power, the regent would no longer take her advice; she became a member of a discontented clique of nobles which was eventually to form the nucleus of one of the Frondes.

Exercise   Review the account of the career of the Duchess of Chevreuse up to 1643 which is given above. Could an analysis of her career be assisted by (a) consideration of how the status of courtiers was determined?; (b) a feminist interpretation?

Discussion   (a)   Marriage alliances with great courtiers like de Luynes and Chevreuse brought with them high prestige and regular proximity to the royal family, especially the queen. In the long run, however, monarchs only gave power to courtiers who furthered royal policies and the duchess spent most of her career doing exactly the opposite. Her importance depended on three factors: her friendship with the queen, her elevated rank as a member of the Guise/Lorraine family and her ability to charm people. By the 1640s age had undermined her capacity to fascinate and circumstances had distanced her from the queen's affections. Rank alone was insufficient to ensure her continued significance.

            (b)   The quotation from Cousin imputes the difficulties of the duchess to her gender and to some failings it was perceived to involve. The extract from Batiffol agrees with the Abbé du Dorat's pejorative verdict on the duchess and dwells on the levity and thoughtlessness of such women. Feminist historians could comment that whilst mischief and folly were often cited as the motivation for female conspirators, men such as Montmorency and Cinq-Mars have often been presented as brave and unfortunate. Their plots have been linked to wider movements against the absolutist policies of the king and cardinal. Those of the duchess have been trivialized although, in several cases, magnates and foreign potentates were associated with her.

Is it possible to discern any clear political objectives in the plots of the Duchess of Chevreuse? Her friendship with the house of Stuart and membership of the house of Lorraine, gave them some consistency but they arose out of personal circumstances. Her influence emanated from her friendship with the queen whose interests could not, in the long run, be disentangled from those of the king. The duchess could only attempt to become a kind of mirror image of Richelieu. If she advised obedience to Louis there was no scope for her personal inclinations, if defiance he could swiftly remove her from the court. Beyond the queen's household, there was no legitimate institutional power base such as the law, army or provincial government which women could use to assert themselves. The cry of the duchess in 1626 that 'people ... thought she was interested only in coquetry, but that she would show them some day that she was capable of other things' encapsulated the dilemma of a strong, intelligent woman with a frustrated drive for political power.

Other female contemporaries of the Duchess of Chevreuse were more successful in achieving influence and even power by less confrontational means. For more about this see Block 2, Unit 6, and Kettering (1989, pp.817–41).

Figure 17
Sir William Alexander, 1st
Earl of Stirling, *engraving
by Bocquet. Mansell
Collection.*

William Alexander, first Earl of Stirling

If you at court to credit would arise,
You must not seek by truth to gain renown,
But sometime must applaud what you despise,
And smile in show whilst in effect you frown.

(McGrail, 1940, p.136)

This was written early in William Alexander's career at court. He had been born into an insignificant gentry family in about 1577 in the village of Menstrie, not far from Stirling. It was adjacent to a seat of the earls of Argyll and he accompanied the young earl on a tour of the continent. This opportunity not only extended his already impressive education but also gave him a powerful nobleman as a patron. He further improved his prospects by marriage to the daughter of the rich and distinguished Sir William Erskine of Balgonie.

William Alexander continued to write poems and prose works throughout his life. He was highly esteemed by contemporaries and was a friend and correspondent of the poet Drummond of Hawthornden. His literary talents would have recommended him to James VI and his sons who all valued the arts. Royal favours began to come his way, probably by means of his father-in-law and the Earl of Argyll. He gained the tenure of Menstrie, continued to acquire lands in the area and undertook various business ventures. By 1609 he had been knighted and made a Gentleman of the Bedchamber Extraordinary to Prince Henry, which meant spending most of his time in England. On the heir's death he entered the service of Prince Charles.

In 1614 Sir William was appointed Master of Requests for Scotland, the king charged him to:

> ... apprehend all those idle and vagrant persons, who coming from thence [Scotland] thither [England], by their misbehaviour here do both trouble us and discredit their country. (McGrail, 1940, p.67)

This was the first of a series of public offices and business ventures which were to alienate Sir William from his countrymen. His importance was confirmed in 1625 when he was made Principal Secretary of State for Scotland, a post he would hold for the next fifteen years until his death. He was based in London except for a few months in the summer which he usually spent in Scotland.

In 1621 he had been appointed, by royal charter, hereditary Lieutenant of the Canadian colony of New Scotland (Nova Scotia):

> To be holden of us from our kingdom of Scotland as a part thereof ... (Rogers, 1877, p.61)

For the next ten years Sir William and his family threw themselves into trying to establish the colony and to make some money out of it. Few Scots were prepared to settle in New Scotland, those that did either died or regretted it. Expensive ships had to be financed to transport and supply them. The Stuarts extended the grant of baronetcies to those who were prepared to invest in the enterprise, the profits were to reimburse Sir William. The new baronets, who enjoyed precedence over older families, were despised and resented in Scotland. As part of the treaty of 1632, Charles ceded New Scotland to France. Sir William was compensated with a grant of £10,000 which he never received, and made a viscount.

The new lord started to build a mansion in Stirling to a design by his second son (see Video 8). A local dissident covered the coat of arms over the entrance, which bore his motto: 'Per Mare, Per Terras', with a dirty cloth bearing the legend: 'Per Metre, Per Turners'. In other words, he had achieved his success by his poems and by issuing copper pennies in Scotland called 'turners' (on which he received a commission). The coronation of Charles in Edinburgh in 1633 brought him more honours including an earldom which he could not really afford to sustain. During the rest of the decade he continued to use his influence at the English court to launch financial schemes, most of which proved unprofitable, and further alienated the Scots.

Stirling's literary skills, his need to make money and unpopular Stuart policies all combined in the affair of King James's psalms. The king had collaborated with the poet to produce a version which he believed to be superior to the popular translation by Sternhold and Hopkins. As an act of filial piety Charles attempted to impose these on his subjects. They got a cool reception in England from Archbishop Laud downwards. Charles persevered in Scotland through the agency of the co-author, Earl William, who was to make a profit from the sales. Scottish churchmen disliked it, mistrusting a courtier who employed ungodly phrases like: 'pale lady of the night'. In 1637 Charles tried to force a new Laudian service book on the Scottish church, to be used in conjunction with King James's psalms. The Earl of Stirling was implicated, as far as his country-men were concerned, in the controversy which led to the breakdown of royal authority in Scotland. By 1638 the king's servants such as the earl, caught in the tension between the force of Scottish resistance and the attempts of Charles to impose his authority from afar, could no longer carry out their duties. Stirling accompanied Charles I to the North in 1639 to face humiliation in the first Bishops' War. He died in London early in the next year heavily burdened with debts.

Exercise   Review the careers of the three nobles outlined above and answer the questions raised at the beginning of this section:

1   What relationship was there between favour at court and a successful career as a magnate?

2   Did the actions of these nobles assist or impede the ability of Charles I and Louis XIII to exercise unlimited power in their states?

Discussion   1   You would preface any generalization about the nobility based on these three cases, with a question about how typical they were of their class. In the case of the Duke of Épernon, he caught the eye of his monarch when he was young and personable. He had great wealth and a substantial clientele, these gave him a power base which made him unwilling automatically to accept royal policies. The Duchess of Chevreuse cannot, perhaps, be compared with the other nobles as her gender did make a difference. For twenty years she was the favourite of the queen of France but shunned by the king. As the queen had little power beyond her own household the duchess built up an alternative source of influence through her friendship with foreign states: Britain, Spain and Lorraine. This forced Louis to treat her with some circumspection. The Earl of Stirling came from obscurity with only his poetry and his complacency to recommend him as a courtier. His attempts to make money and the erection of his mansion in Stirling only led to his greater unpopularity in Scotland and, ultimately, to bankruptcy.

2   The courts of Charles I and Louis XIII were similar in many respects even to the way in which the households were structured and their ceremonial life conducted. Both monarchs regarded their courts as extensions of their own personalities and preferences, as agencies through which their policies could be demonstrated and, to a large extent, implemented. Their great nobles played a vital part in this process.

     The Duke of Épernon and the Duchess of Chevreuse were not chosen by Louis as favourites. He inherited the former and the latter was foisted on him by her two great marriages. The duke seldom attended court, his representative was his son, the Cardinal de la Valette, who did his best to safeguard family interests. When Épernon exasperated Louis and Richelieu beyond forgiveness, they had no difficulty in destroying him because the nobility had been cowed by twenty years of the increasingly successful assertion of royal power. Her connections allowed the Duchess of Chevreuse to cause the king embarrassment whether she was at court or in exile. Once she lost the favour of Anne of Austria her standing was fatally impaired.

     The Earl of Stirling had been 'made' at the English court and felt the need to safeguard and enhance his position there in the king's presence. He would have been more useful to Charles if he had spent his time in Scotland, furthering his business enterprises and establishing a supportive clientele

     Both monarchs recognized the political importance of their nobility and protected or enhanced the prestige of those who were loyal. They attempted to ensure the obedience of magnates in the regions, but Louis was more effective in imposing his will throughout his kingdom.

Before you decide if Starkey's dictum that: 'the King's Court *was* the government', has been validated by the evidence discussed so far, it would be wise to consider the legal and political institutions in the British Isles and France, religious problems and interests which were not directly dependent on the royal will. All were to contribute to a crisis, for both monarchies, during the middle years of the century.

Finance and administration

The view of monarchy which was conveyed by the ceremonies and entertainments at the English and French courts was one where the king's virtue and wisdom justified the exercise of considerable personal power (prerogative). You will already have gathered that these claims were frequently contested; in France as often as in Britain. This final part of the unit looks at how and why royal policies were questioned and estimates how successful they had been by the 1640s.

In the British Isles and France there were three main areas of potential conflict between the kings and their subjects: powerful ministers and favourites, taxes and religion. We have seen above some of the ways in which ministers and favourites, who were personal servants of the crown and members of the court, could achieve power. Perhaps Louis XIII showed his superior capacities as a king by shunning favourites after the death of de Luynes, utilizing instead the formidable abilities of his chief minister, Richelieu. The reliance Charles I placed on his unpopular favourite Buckingham during the early years of his reign contributed to his showdown with parliament over religious policy and taxation in 1629. The king's subsequent employment of Wentworth, first as President of the Council of the North and then in Ireland, probably looked, in the early years, like an effective means of asserting royal authority. But Wentworth (later Earl of Strafford) had neither the intellectual capacity nor the high standing of Richelieu. Worst of all, he served a king whose religious views differed from the majority of his subjects in Scotland and Ireland and from many of his English subjects. Louis XIII and Richelieu, on the other hand, successfully deprived their Huguenot minority (about 6–7% of the population) of independent political power during the 1620s and experienced very little trouble from them subsequently. They also supported the spirit of the decrees of the Council of Trent which confirmed the strength and orthodoxy of the Catholic Church in France and the loyalty of its clergy.

Louis XIII and Charles were faced with the same financial problems. Both received revenue from their own lands and from legal fines and customs dues. Rents and fines were often fixed at traditional levels, market prices rose and fell, but mostly they rose. Customs dues could and did increase but only when trade was buoyant. Both kings could lawfully ask their subjects for additional taxes (often called subsidies in England). When they were waging war, as they frequently were during this period, the financial strain on their resources became acute and the need for higher and more taxes urgent. The main French tax, the *taille* was fixed and levied in ways which differed from one region to another (see Briggs, p.229) and provided plenty of scope for conflict between the king and his people.

Exercise   Read *Anthology* I.11 and re-read Briggs pp.95–9.
What were the major problems that Richelieu and Louis XIII encountered in raising taxation and how did they cope with them?

Discussion   The king and his minister inherited a system which was burdened with vested interests. The pressure of war and lack of co-operation by the

Parlements and financiers caused reform initiatives to founder. Marillac in his letter to Richelieu described a bargain by which the deputies of Burgundy were trying to buy off the king. The deal was that, in return for 1.8 million livres, he would allow them to keep their traditional method of raising taxation, by decision of the provincial estates, rather than by giving that power to *élections*, a court of venal officials appointed by the king. Although Marillac implied that the king was inflexible, Briggs p.97, gives a rather different account of what usually happened in such cases: '... a repeated pattern of exaggerated royal demands, followed by threats of resistance and negotiations, ending in substantial modifications to the original proposals'.

In the second part of *Anthology*, I.11, Marillac referred to the king's decision to end the *droit annuel* or *paulette* for judicial office-holders (see Unit 1). This, like the spasmodic attempts to replace provincial estates by *élections* as the taxing authorities, was part of a coherent programme of reforms which some historians have attributed to Louis XIII and Richelieu (e.g. Kierstead, 1975, pp.25–39). Robin Briggs (1992, pp.71–97) finds little evidence to support such a claim. The introduction of *intendants*, directly appointed royal officials, who progressively tightened the grip of the state on the provinces, was a much more important development than half-baked fiscal initiatives (see Briggs, pp.119–21).

> Although war may have involved great suffering and terrible risks, the morally inconvenient truth is that the state would emerge from it enormously strengthened, if also deeply flawed in its underlying fiscal and social structure. (Briggs, 1992, p.97)

The progressive introduction of the institutions of an absolute monarchy was not accomplished without opposition (see Briggs, pp. 114–24). You have read in the last exercise about the revolts in Dijon and Aix of the *lanturlus* (the refrain of a subversive popular song) and the *cascaveaux* (rebels were issued with little bells which they rang violently to annoy their enemies) on behalf of provincial liberties. You will see from the map (Briggs, p.115) that these were by no means the last acts of defiance against the government. Popular revolts often occurred because taxes fell most heavily on the third estate and upon the common people and were increased to pay for the maintenance of order and foreign wars. The 1630s were a period of particular hardship caused by harvest failures, plague and the decline of trade; the country was troubled by beggars, vagrants and deserters. The revolt of the Nu-Pieds (bare-foots) in Normandy in 1639 was a larger and more concentrated example of the kind of protest which had existed throughout the decade.

When the peasants combined with the urban workers and, in some cases, the bourgeoisie and office-holders, the situation became more dangerous. In Bordeaux in 1635, for example, attempts to levy tax on wine and on barrels led to an innkeepers' and coopers' revolt which was initially welcomed by the office-holders. Eventually the kind of compromises described by Briggs (p.97) were normally concluded. Most dangerous of all was the opposition of the nobility, not all of whom were rich and powerful; for example in Brittany there were, perhaps, ten thousand noble families, many with estates of no more than 20 hectares (40 acres). As Devon remarks:

> ... there existed in the middle of the seventeenth century a sort of noble proletariat, an inexhaustible reserve of men for all the trouble-makers ... (Devon, 1975, p.35)

You have read above of the repeated involvement of the king's younger brother, Gaston of Orléans, and nobles like the Duchess of Chevreuse, in conspiracies and rebellions. Fortunately for the monarchy, even during the period of the Frondes, the interests of the peasants, urban workers, bourgeoisie, venal office-holders, 'noble proletariat' and great nobles never coalesced to support clearly defined anti-monarchical policies as they did in contemporary England.

Charles I was king of England, king of Scotland and king of Ireland and, impressive as these titles sound, his multiple kingdoms caused some of his worst problems. Russell (1990) identifies the 'British dimension' as a factor which exacerbated the difficulties the king and his ministers had in implementing religious and fiscal policies.

In the *Anthology* (I.7) you read the nervous self-justifications offered by Strafford to his friend, Archbishop Laud, defending his aggrandisement as Lord Deputy in Ireland against the accusations of his enemies. His anxiety in 1637, well before royal authority was to break down in Ireland, showed some awareness of his problems.

Exercise   Read Coward, pp.127 and 171–2.
Assess the strengths and weaknesses of Strafford's rule in Ireland.

Discussion   Ironically the presence of so many 'New English' settlers, which was perceived to be a source of strength for the royal administration, was to prove disastrous. The new impetus which Strafford's energetic policy of 'thorough' was to give the plantation of Ireland, was to increase the desperation of the native, marginalized Irish and finally lead to their rebellion. The 'Old English' who were mainly Catholics and therefore, second-class citizens in the state, resented both the plantations and the recusancy fines which weakened them economically.

The 'New English', who were economically the most powerful class in Ireland, were progressively alienated by Strafford's fiscal and religious policies. The revival of the fines levied by the courts of wards and liveries, the enforcement of a Statute of Uses and the resumption of land which had once belonged to the church, hurt the 'New English' in their most tender spot, their purses. The attempt to impose Charles I's and Laud's Arminian brand of Anglicanism through the hated Court of High Commission further exasperated the settlers.

Strafford was extremely successful in increasing royal revenues and in asserting the king's power in Ireland. Yet, in the long run, his achievements were symbolized by his palace at Jigginstown, ambitious, imposing but ruined before it was completed. (See TV2.)

Kearney (1989) identifies three ways in which Strafford was both a reformer and the architect of the destruction of royal authority in 1640. For the first time there was:

> ... an attempt by a prominent member of the English privy council at direct colonial administration of the whole island. Unlike his immediate predecessors, Strafford was an important English politician in his own right and he enjoyed the confidence of the king and of Laud throughout his whole period of office ...
>
> For the first time since the later middle ages, the English government was not called upon to make a substantial contribution to the Irish exchequer or to give way on important issues in return for a subsidy from the Irish parliament. Strafford was successful ... in solving the financial problem and it was this success which made possible the freedom of action enjoyed by the administration in these years ...
>
> For the first time since the Reformation the persecution of Protestants took place in Ireland at the hands of the Court of High Commission. ... Over doctrine, discipline and the resumption of church lands and impropriate livings [benefices held by laymen], Strafford aroused the sternest opposition ... (Kearney, 1989, pp.217–18)

Was it the very strength of Stuart rule in Ireland and Scotland, the fact that it did not have to make concessions on 'important issues', that led to its destruction? Mitchison (1983) characterizes Scotland after 1603 as being governed 'by the pen'. Royal authority was enhanced by the physical removal of the kingly body four hundred miles southward. No longer could the Scots nobility and Calvinist divines hector and dominate the monarch as they had done in the days of Mary, Queen of Scots and the young James VI. As James I of England he had gained considerable prestige with his Scots subjects by his new wealth and importance. He ruled them reasonably effectively at a distance through a privy council of ageing peers, civil servants and a complacent parliament, and did not press conformity on the Presbyterian majority. The Catholic minority, who were mainly highland clansmen, continued to be doubly penalized: despised and persecuted.

Exercise   Read Coward, pp.178–80 and re-read pp.55–7, above on the Earl of Stirling. How far were Charles I's policies in Scotland responsible for the outbreak of war in 1639?

Discussion   Coward firmly places responsibility for the outbreak of war with Charles I. His remoteness from Scottish life and values prevented him from realizing how unrealistic his policies were. Anglicized advisers like the Earl of Stirling were little better placed to know the true state of affairs. He usually spent a few weeks in Scotland annually and annoyed his countrymen by his pretentious lifestyle whilst he was there. Privileges such as the monopoly of issuing small coins (turners) and the sale of baronetcies whose holders enjoyed precedence over older families, were bitterly resented. The support of such royal favourites proved useless when the crisis came.

The ill-advised policy of revoking royal and kirk gifts proved very unpopular. Worse still, Charles directed hostility towards his Scots bishops who had, up until the 1630s, been tolerated by moderate Presbyterians. By using them in his government and as a means of enforcing an Arminian form of worship, he caused a reaction which ended in the signing of the Covenant. The fiasco of the attempted imposition of the Anglican prayer book initiated a series of violent acts of defiance against the king which culminated in war.

The growing hatred of the policies of Charles I in England and Scotland cannot be separated. The opposition to his absolutist tendencies inside and outside of the English parliament which, in any case, shared many grievances with the Scots, took comfort from their effective resistance to the royal will. Similarly, the Scots might not have been so ready to make war had they believed that Charles was enthusiastically supported by the majority of his English subjects.

Exercise   Read Coward, pp.166–78.

1   Were there any positive aspects of the 'personal rule'?

2   What were the main sources of conflict between Charles I and his subjects, 1629–40?

Discussion 1   Coward concedes that Charles and his ministers made real attempts to achieve reforms and warns against the dangers of assuming that, since a civil war did eventually break out in which he was defeated, that was the inevitable conclusion to his reign. Withdrawal from the Thirty Years' War and the careful policies of Weston stabilized the financial situation in the early 1630s. The issue of the Books of Orders in times of hardship by centrally appointed commissioners showed the state's concern for the poor.

2   Fiscal measures initially caused annoyance rather than violent opposition. The distraint of knighthood, the granting of some monopolies, the revival of forest courts and even the extension of Ship Money in 1635 to inland counties, aroused little serious opposition. Large-scale refusals to pay the tax coincided with the outbreak of the first Bishops' War when Englishmen were dividing for and against the king's authority.

Some of the measures which Laud insisted on taking: the railing of altars which were to be at the east end of churches, the encouragement of sports on the Sabbath, an emphasis on works rather than on the scriptures, all smacked of popery. This impression was re-inforced by the influence enjoyed by Charles's Catholic queen and the continental tastes blatantly cultivated at his court. The imposition of most of the regulations concerning religion were visible at local level: the omnipresence of the authority of the Court of High Commission was a further source of aggravation. The unease of many of the propertied classes at the way in which the new religious policies were undermining their local status and interests gave leaders to the growing movement of opinion against such state intervention.

Until 1642 English resistance to royal policy did not extend to violence. Most of the gentry strongly identified with their locality and, as justices of the peace, were often involved in its administration. Opposition to the royal government was run by skilful political operators using parliament and the law courts. So what actually drove a large cross-section of the nation to serious resistance? Morrill (1984, p.157) suggests that it was not the legal-constitutionalist arguments or the level of unparliamentary taxation which convinced people that they should rebel. It was 'the force of religion that drove minorities to fight and forced majorities to make reluctant choices'.

Serious challenges to state power were to be made in France and the British Isles during the middle decades of the seventeenth century. They were ultimately ineffective in France where, progressively, control of the regions had passed from the magnates and assemblies to royal officials, especially the ·*intendants*. The great majority in France shared a common fidelity to the Catholic Church and this worked in favour of the highly orthodox monarchy. In England much of the local government was conducted by justices of the peace, mostly drawn from the local gentry. They were a class which increasingly saw parliament as an institution of the state which was an equal or superior partner to an unreasonable king. When the religion that he tried to enforce diverged seriously from that of many of his English and most of his Scottish subjects, the gentry already had an alternative source of authority in parliament behind which they could marshal their forces.

References

Asch, R.G. (1991), 'The Revival of Monopolies: Court and Patronage during the personal rule of Charles I, 1629–1640', in R.G. Asch and A.M. Birke (eds), *Princes, Patronage and Nobility*, Studies of the German Historical Institute, Oxford University Press, London.

Batiffol, L. (1913), *The Duchesse de Chevreuse*, William Heinemann, London.

Briggs, R. (1992), 'Richelieu and Reform', in J. Bergin and L.W.B. Brockliss (eds), *Richelieu and his Age*, Oxford University Press, Oxford.

Cousin, V. (1859), *Secret History of the French Court Richelieu and Mazarin: or Life and times of Madame de Chevreuse*, trans. M.L. Booth, Delisser and Procter, New York.

Devon, P. (1975) 'Relations between the French nobility and the Absolute Monarchy in the First Half of the Seventeenth Century', in R.F. Kierstead (ed.), pp.25–39.

Evans, R.J.W., 'The Court: A Protean Institution and an Elusive Subject', in R.G. Asch and A.M. Birke (eds), *Princes, Patronage and Nobility*, Studies of the German Historical Institute, Oxford University Press, London.

Fessenden, N.B. (1972), 'Épernon and Guyenne', an unpublished Ph.D. thesis, Columbia University.

Kearney, H. (1989), *Strafford in Ireland, 1633–41: a Study in Absolutism*, Cambridge University Press, Cambridge.

Kettering, S. (1986), *Patrons, Brokers and Clients in Seventeenth Century France*, Oxford University Press, Oxford.

Kettering, S. (1989), 'The patronage power of early modern French noble women', *Historical Journal*, 32, pp.817–41.

Kierstead, R.F. (ed.) (1975), *State and Society in Seventeenth Century France*, New Viewpoints, New York.

Lavollée, R. (ed.) (1925), *Mémoires du Cardinal de Richelieu*, vol.6, Société de l'Histoire de France, Édouard Champion, Paris.

McGrail, T.H. (1940), *Sir William Alexander. First Earl of Stirling*, Oliver and Boyd, Edinburgh.

Mitchison, R. (1983), *Lordship to Patronage: Scotland 1603–1745*, Edward Arnold, London.

Moote, A.L. (1989), *Louis the Just*, University of California Press, California.

Morrill, J. (1984), 'The religious context of the English civil war', *Transactions of the Royal Historical Society*, 5th ser., 34, pp.155–78.

Ollard, R. (1979), *The Image of the King: Charles I and Charles II*, Hodder and Stoughton, London.

Pickel, M.B. (1936), *Charles I as Patron of Poetry and Drama*, Frederick Muller, London.

Rogers, C. (1877), *Memorials of the Earl of Stirling and of the House of Alexander*, vol. 1, Edinburgh.

Russell, C. (1990), *The Causes of the English Civil War: the Ford lectures delivered in the University of Oxford, 1987–88*, Clarendon Press, Oxford.

Starkey, D. (ed.) (1987), *The English Court: From the Wars of the Roses to the Civil War*, Longman, London.

Unit 3
The Civil War in the British Isles and the Frondes in France

Prepared for the course team by Henry Cowper and Ian Donnachie

Contents

Study timetable

Weeks of study	Texts	Video	AC	Set books
2	Unit 3, *Anthology*, I.12–17, Illustration Book, Offprint 4, Offprint R. Knecht *The Fronde*	Video 3	AC1, section 2	Coward, Briggs', Date Chart

During the period of this unit you should also watch TV5 and 6.

Objectives

To help you to:

1   understand the main causes of unrest leading to the civil wars in England, Scotland and Ireland from 1640 and the circumstances surrounding the revolts associated with the crisis of 1648 and the subsequent Fronde of the nobles in France continuing to 1652–3;

2   unravel the key issues of the civil wars in the British Isles and in France;

3   compare and contrast the origins, nature, participants, their differing and changing objectives and outcome of the two conflicts;

4   assess briefly the immediate results in each case.

Before starting work on this unit you should read Bonney (Offprint 4), Coward, chapter 6 and Briggs, pp.105–34. In addition to the set reading for this unit, you should read the separate offprint by R.J. Knecht on the Fronde (Professor Knecht uses the singular form). This article, originally published as a Historical Association pamphlet, sets out rather more clearly than does Briggs an account of the Frondes, comparable to the account of the English civil war in Chapter 6 of Coward.

Introduction

Probably the most important events in the British Isles and France during this period were the civil wars and the rebellions associated with the protest movement known as the Frondes, from the French for a sling used by children – and hence a pejorative term describing the disaffected projecting stones at their enemies or their property. It's quite likely that you'll know something about the causes, events and consequences of the civil wars in England between 1642 and 1648, but are likely to be less familiar with the situation in the other countries of the British Isles (which impinged significantly on the English experience) or the roughly contemporaneous, though apparently not quite so dramatic, events on the other side of the Channel associated with the Frondes in the years 1648–53.

The causes of civil strife in the 1640s and 1650s

In Unit 2 we saw how relations between kings, ministers and subjects were deteriorating in the 1630s. Dramatic historical events like the civil wars and the strife associated with the Frondes neither occurred in a vacuum, nor by accident. Force of circumstances had some part in the proceedings, but in general the events in both the British Isles and France can be explained by one or other of two sets of causes: long-term factors; and, short-term factors.

The long-term factors, such as wars (specifically the Thirty Years' War, 1618–48), economic conditions, social changes, political representation, and religious grievances, often dating back several generations, set the context for unrest and upheaval in the British Isles and France.

Short-term factors were often closely associated with the actions of the executive relative to parliament and the church, as well as the omnipresent issue of taxation, which affected the economic position of many social groups in both the British Isles and France. In England, for example, the most important issue about taxation was that the king's normal income wasn't sufficient to support the routine costs of government in peacetime, let alone in a period of war. An earlier indication of how foreign policy could influence developments on the domestic front in this regard was English participation in the Thirty Years' War during the 1620s, when taxation to pay for the war began to emerge as a major political issue. Underlying grievances about taxation surfaced again during the Bishops' War against the Scots (1639–40) and then with the outbreak of a major rebellion in Ireland in 1641. For France, more closely embroiled than England, the Thirty Years' War proved enormously expensive financially and in human terms.

Clearly long- and short-term factors were often closely related, as, for example, the attempts of both executives to raise income through taxation from people whose ability or inability to pay was much influenced by both long- and short-term economic forces. So this makes it difficult to disentangle immediate causes close to the events from those at some remove. And, although we talk as if we are dealing with two countries, in reality it's four or even five – with distinctive economic, social, political and religious characteristics and considerable regional diversity within their boundaries.

England and Wales seem at first glance to have been the most cohesive of the countries, but there were also considerable regional differences – as for example between London and the provinces, or more generally between town and countryside. Wales had its own particular identity; its culture and language gave it an essentially Celtic character. Unlike Ireland and Scotland, Wales had been most closely integrated politically with England – a situation formalized in 1536 when the principality was united with its larger and more powerful neighbour.

In Ireland the situation was complicated by the long-term overlay of English and Scottish settlement on Irish lands, particularly on the northern and eastern seaboard. In many parts of the island the Irish language and culture prevailed as did native Irish land ownership and Catholicism. But as we will see later in the unit, the Irish felt increasingly threatened by the relentless western march of English settlement. Just to make matters more complicated, in the aftermath of the Reformation religious differences became more sharply defined as between Catholics (the majority and including some 'Old English' long-term settlers) and Protestants (the minority). This was perhaps most apparent in Ulster where Scottish Presbyterians had been encouraged to settle under a series of 'plantation' schemes formulated by James VI and I, (see TV3).

Across the North Channel, as you'll recall from Unit 1, Scotland, after the Union of the Crowns in 1603, shared its monarch with England, but still retained its own parliament in Edinburgh, its legal system and its kirk. Despite the union there was deep-seated mistrust of everything English, particularly what was seen as a dangerous equivocation about religion. Presbyterianism, firmly rooted in Calvinist theology, was much stronger in Scotland. Unlike English bishops, who were considered (though not by Puritans) to hold their offices by apostolic succession, Scottish bishops were perceived as little more than ecclesiastical officials. The close association between kirk and state meant that many of the political differences between Scotland and England centred around this specific issue. For example, one of the issues which most undermined the Anglo-Scottish alliance of 1643 was the issue of 'Erastianism', or lay control of the kirk. The Scots wanted lay involvement through the General Assembly of the kirk, and bitterly opposed government control. They regarded the Assembly as answerable only to God. In England, however, the Church of England was subject to parliament in a number of issues and bishops sat in the House of Lords.

Early seventeenth-century France, as you can see from the map in Briggs (p.xii), had different boundaries from the present day and some of these counted for more even than those outlined in the British Isles. The outlying provinces all had privileges which to greater or lesser extent shielded them from direct rule by the French crown. France was a much larger country than any of its cross-Channel neighbours and exhibited many distinctive regional and cultural differences (e.g. in western parts of

Brittany, Breton was the principal language and the culture remained rooted in the Celtic tradition). The French king was obliged to respect provincial particularism in a much more profound sense than the king of England. The sheer size of France gave rise to major problems of communication and administration hence the monarchy's grip on the reigns of power was often tenuous.

Exercise On the basis of the discussion above what major political problems did the monarchies on either side of the Channel share?

Discussion Internally both monarchies were facing increasing financial problems, having to pay for expensive wars, and resorting to unpopular taxation to raise the necessary revenue. Resentment of royal authority on a number of other issues was also growing – particularly in the component nations and provinces. These two fundamental problems linked to the major external issue – participation in the Thirty Years' War (though note that the English war against France ended in 1629 and that against Spain in 1630).

Causes of the civil wars in the British Isles

Start by reading pp.185–9 of Coward, where there is a useful discussion of the origins of the English civil wars.

You only have to read these first few pages of Coward's chapter to see that the causes of the 'English Revolution' and the civil strife that accompanied it have generated considerable historical debate. Some historians see the English civil war as part of an evolutionary process, part of long-term changes in the economy, the social structure and in politics. Other historians see it in terms of a shorter-term breakdown in the constitution in which the personality of Charles I and his financial mismanagement were the real catalysts to war. This second group are known as the 'revisionists'. We shall look at these different approaches in Unit 4. The search for explanations for the outbreak of the civil wars in the 1640s continues, especially with detailed examination of the background in each of the countries in the 'multiple kingdom' of England and Wales, Scotland and Ireland. Just as critical is knowing more about what happened in localities and the role played by different social groups. However, there is still no right answer to the question of the origins of the civil wars.

The context of the civil wars

We shall now examine the context in which the civil strife was set. As suggested above, four major long-term factors (i.e. economic, social, political and religious changes and grievances) need to be considered before we look at explanations more immediately related to the events of the 1640s. Let us now look at England.

Economic factors

England's economy, like that of France, Scotland and Ireland, was still heavily dependent on agriculture, which occupied the majority of the population and created between 75 and 80 per cent of the country's wealth. In England, and to a lesser extent Scotland and Ireland, the economy was subject to considerable changes and stresses due to new modes of agricultural production, early manifestations of industrialization, and changing patterns of domestic and overseas trade. Underpinning these difficulties was the fundamental problem of price rises, which had been a prominent feature of the economy for nearly a century, and had been seen at its worst in the great leap in food prices which occurred in the 1590s due to a series of bad harvests.

Although still a matter of historical debate, it seems that this long-term rise in prices can be explained by the partial failure of agriculture to meet the needs of a rising and increasingly urbanized population, even though only about 20 per cent lived in towns. While the implementation of widespread agricultural enclosure and drainage schemes held out the possibility of enhanced productivity in the longer term, such developments were, in the short term, highly disruptive economically and socially because they alienated many poorer people and sometimes led to village revolts as in the Fenland. Output was also drastically affected by a series of bad harvests and particularly severe crises during the early 1620s, 1630s and the later 1640s. The last came very soon after a particularly bad trade depression during 1640–2.

Industry was also experiencing the strains and stresses of a period when new technology was challenging the old, particularly traditional forms of production. English technology and manufacturing, especially iron-making, mining and textiles, were relatively backward compared with techniques prevailing on the continent. However, there was a rapid catching-up process in the later Tudor and early Stuart era, sufficient enough in its impact to be described by some earlier historians as an 'industrial revolution'. It brought its problems because when the technological gap between England and the continent had been closed, coal and iron output seems to have fallen. More important, the great English staple, cloth production, was also a victim of changing technology. Although this period saw the successful establishment of 'new draperies', traditional broadcloth production was badly affected, especially in the West Country in the early 1640s.

There were other problems for both trade and manufacturing caused by monopolistic restrictions and poor transport. Government intervention in economic affairs was more motivated by the immediate financial needs of the crown than the national interest. Royal monopolies, giving a single individual or company sole control over the entire production of a good or service, introduced under the Tudors, continued to operate over certain spheres of trade, industry and mining. Merchant adventurers had to pay handsomely for the privilege. Certainly, according to the latest evidence, it's hard to prove that industrial output increased or that living standards were much enhanced by such economic growth as occurred before the civil war.

Note too that increased urbanization, which involved migration from the countryside and from villages and smaller towns to the larger centres, inevitably brought about economic stresses. This development – also seen in France – was characterized in England by the growth of London. Some of the English ports were actually adversely affected by the enhancement of London's trade, and inland centres suffered from shifts in industry. Industrial inertia did not save them and industry, in any case, was still widely dispersed throughout the countryside rather than concentrated in towns. (AC1, section 1 discusses land use and distribution of population.)

Social factors

As Coward says, there are some problems for the historian of social change in the early Stuart period due to the limitations in primary sources, including huge gaps in the record and very limited and inconsistent data. Nevertheless we can still see stresses appearing in the social structure and various social problems which contributed to tension before the civil wars.

In descending order of economic fortunes and standards of living were the aristocracy, gentry, yeoman, urban freemen, labourers (rural and urban), and at the bottom of the heap, vagrants. Inevitably, as in France, there was massively unequal wealth between such social groupings and considerable regional disparities. But, again as in France, all were affected by price rises.

The landowning classes experienced mixed fortunes – a reflection of the periodic crises that hit agriculture during the first half of the seventeenth century. Taxation was lower in England than in France and was more easily collected until the 1630s, when fierce objections to Charles I's financial expedients were registered. The problem wasn't just taxes, it was the declining value of rents and the increasing difficulty of getting people to pay them. Altogether different was the position of those who actually lived on the land and worked it, the labourers, who made up to anything between one-quarter and one-third of the total population, and whose standard of living was falling drastically because of price rises. Hence the problem of poverty, already deep-rooted, was greatly increasing, with many slipping into vagrancy. Rising numbers of poor raised the spectre of civil disorder in the government and more generally fear of poverty and the impoverished was widespread and growing.

The same disparities existed in the towns, where much of the wealth was concentrated in the hands of an urban élite. This does not deny the fact that, with the growth of towns, wealth was trickling down to an urban lower class, mainly small merchants and craftsmen. But at the same time guilds and trades, as in most times of economic hardship, were becoming increasingly exclusive and defensive of their rights and privileges – thus causing further frustration at this level of society. In England, as in France, economic grievances and fear of change could readily be related to political and religious grievances.

Exercise   Summarize the relationship between the economy and the social conditions described above.

Discussion   This is by no means easy and we have to bear in mind that much of what has been discussed remains contentious. But basically the economic problems of the period, both long and short term, can be seen to underpin the social problems, affecting the fortunes of all social groups, and causing greater social tension.

Political and religious factors

The majority of the longer-term political causes of the civil war are closely identified with the extra-parliamentary and parliamentary challenges to the rule of Charles I, whose exercise of the royal prerogative from the moment of his succession in 1625 seemed quickly to extend 'beyond its just symmetry' in both political and religious spheres.

The complex activities of Charles's government and especially the period of his personal rule 1629–40 hold the key to explaining the context in which the constitutional crisis of November 1640 to September 1641 and ultimately the first civil war itself occurred. The main facets of the personal rule have been covered in Unit 2 so look back at the discussion there to remind yourself of the main issues.

Undoubtedly the major problem was the increasing financial difficulty of the crown to meet the ordinary expenses of government which meant resort to new and higher levels of taxation to pay for wars (see Coward, pp.166–9). Forced loans, militia payments and the enforced billeting of troops were much resented. Attempts to reform the militia were also regarded with suspicion. The payment of the infamous ship money was resisted in some places.

Even after withdrawal from the Thirty Years' War in 1629–30, which ought to have reduced expenditure, taxation was extended. After 1630 the land tax appeared more permanent and in 1635 demands for ship money were extended to certain inland counties, where, not surprisingly, opposition soon reached down the social scale – even below the freeholder class. The legality of the levy was challenged in 1637 by John Hampden, a Buckinghamshire gentleman, and as you can see from the following exercise the case had much wider concerns than ship money.

Exercise   Read *Anthology*, I.12 and briefly summarize the points made about the relationship between king and parliament.

Discussion   The speech states the constitutional position of king and parliament, stressing the important role of the latter because it is representative of the whole kingdom, is a forum for complaints, discusses a wide range of concerns, and passes laws of universal benefit. St John challenges the king's personal rule, particularly his right to raise 'supply' through taxation, which ought to be a matter for parliament to decide. The bringing of the case itself was highly significant and also important was the use of the law courts as means of objecting to royal policy when parliament was not sitting.

Despite growing discontent, it is evidence of the success of the king's financial expedients that he was able to pay for the first campaign in the Bishops' Wars (1639) without parliament. It was the likelihood of a second war against the Scots which really led to the calling of the Short Parliament. The first campaign had emptied the exchequer and even though royal revenue had increased in the 1630s, and probably did cover the ordinary expenses of government by the end of the decade, it was the extraordinary expense of a war which led to the need to call parliament.

Another major issue was the king's devotion to religious ideas and practices which highlighted the sacramental and ceremonial aspects of the church service (see Coward, pp.172–8). These smacked of popery and challenged the views of many of his subjects, at least in England and Scotland. The attempts to impose greater uniformity on the church and the increasing lack of toleration of Puritans within the church was much resented. Laud's reforms were seen as creeping Catholicism – not only in England, but more critically, as discussed below, in Scotland and to a lesser degree amongst the Protestant landlord class in Ireland.

The Scottish revolution

Some would claim that the immediate origins of the English civil wars lay in what is generally described as the 'Scottish Revolution' of 1637–40. Certainly it acted as a trigger to events in England.

Exercise   Read Coward (pp.178–80) and, using the date chart, summarize the main events leading to rebellion in Scotland.

Discussion   Your response should include the important point that the king, out of touch with Scottish opinion, attempted to impose new policies on landowners and the kirk. The first, announced in 1625, would confirm earlier royal gifts of property in return for financial compensation to the crown; the second, dated 1633, was altogether more contentious since it challenged both kirk government and commonly held religious practice. The attempt to introduce the English Prayer Book in 1637 provoked powerful nationalist and religious opposition and in the associated riots women played a significant role. From widespread protest grew the petitioning movement and a permanent representative body which drew up the National Covenant of 1638 and ultimately led to war.

Figure 18
Riot in St Giles' church,
Edinburgh, 1637. Jenny Geddes
aims a stool at the Minister's
head. Engraving attributed to
Hollar. Reproduced from A
Picture History of British
History, vol.2 1485–1688,
1915, Cambridge University
Press.

Let's look in greater detail at these events which seem to indicate that the reaction against royal authority became more aggressive with every move Charles made. Although born in Dunfermline, Charles only visited his northern realm twice when he was king. In 1633 he went to Edinburgh for his long-delayed coronation, returning in 1641 to participate in the event known as the 'Incident', an unsuccessful attempt at undermining the position of his Scottish adversaries. In his absence the policies he promoted provoked growing antagonism towards the crown from an increasingly wide spectrum of the population. Landowners and the nobility in particular were greatly perturbed by the Act of Revocation of 1625, which seemed to endanger their rights to former church properties which had been in their possession since the 1540s. Charles did not seriously intend wholesale denudation of these acquisitions but merely wished to improve the financial status of the post-Reformation church. Royal income would also benefit in a modest way as well. But the whole business was tackled badly causing widespread suspicion and resentment among an influential group in the community. The revocation of certain hereditary sheriffdoms held by some of the most powerful families and an apparent preference for ecclesiastical councillors – Archbishop Sharp, appointed chancellor in 1635 was the first post-Reformation churchman to hold such a position – were political grievances to augment those concerning property among the nobility.

Also, regular taxation, begun by James VI and continued by Charles, was particularly contentious. The king only requested contributions from the Scots in 1625, 1630, and 1633 but since these grants were spread over four years they virtually amounted to annual taxation. Moreover, a larger proportion of the population was affected since his father's expedient of taxing annual rents was extended. Linked to the general disgruntlement over fiscal policy were grievances peculiar to Edinburgh, whose citizens were unenthusiastic about paying for the king's coronation, with its unfamiliar and unpopular Anglican ritual. Nor did they approve of increasing ministers' stipends in the city. But the major objection was having to bear the expense of a new parliament house that Charles wished to build in the capital and ultimately cost £127,000.

However, it was the king's religious innovations that effectively united most of the country against the crown. The Anglican-inspired Book of Canons, to accompany the liturgy (1636) and the Prayer Book itself (1637), provoked a serious reaction throughout much of the country, notably the celebrated riot within St Giles, the capital's cathedral. Charles refused to acknowledge the mounting criticism of his policies, hence the drawing up of the National Covenant, a key document in the history of seventeenth-century Scotland. It was signed on 28 February and 1 March 1638 by various prominent magnates, lairds, ministers and burgesses before being distributed for general subscription throughout the country.

Exercise   Read *Anthology*, I.13, and comment on the general tone, and to whom you think it is addressed.

Discussion   The tone and style are dogmatic and strident and the document is clearly designed for public consumption, and it is apparent that the covenant is articulated on behalf of all classes, including burgesses and 'commons'. Indirectly it is addressed to the king. Throughout there is skilful reference to previous enactments which had bound the king's father, James VI, to the 'true religion' and to the practices dictated by the reformers for the defence of the faith. The National Covenant stresses that Charles should consult parliament and the church rather than behave in an arbitrary manner.

The signatories also pledged themselves to ignore and resist the religious changes introduced by the crown until such time as they could be discussed by a General Assembly of the kirk and by parliament. Such was the nationwide support for the Covenant that Charles back-pedalled and permitted the kirk to hold a General Assembly in Glasgow in 1638. The decisions taken there were to lead to a complete breakdown of relations between Charles and his Scottish subjects. The abolition of episcopacy was a direct challenge to royal authority and both sides were soon preparing for war. Ultimately, as you can see from your reading of Coward, the Scots were powerful and it was the crisis caused by the Bishops' Wars and the invasion of England by the Scots that resulted in Charles being forced to raise an army without any money to pay for it and thus having to call the Short Parliament and then the Long Parliament in 1640. As the situation deteriorated in England the king had little alternative but to sign the Treaty of Ripon (1640) ending the second Bishops' War and submitting to its humiliating terms. Coward (pp.197–9) describes the failed counter-revolutionary 'Incident', which occurred during Charles's second visit in the autumn of 1641, and destroyed any hopes he might have had of raising support in Scotland.

The immediate pre–war crisis in England

In England, the prevailing climate was also one of resentment over long-term grievances while the financial impositions of the crown and a lack of enthusiasm for a Scottish war, or the expense of an army to suppress the rebellion in Ireland, which broke out in October 1641, helped to trigger events immediately preceding the civil war. Popery was greatly feared, but the idea took hold, as relations between king and parliament deteriorated, that Charles might use the army raised to suppress the Irish rebellion against parliament in London.

   Coward (pp.189–97) summarizes the main events in the confrontation between king and parliament, showing how the initial unity that prevailed among the parliamentarians gave way to disagreements, and how the king attempted to capitalize on the discord and uncertainty, not only in England itself, but also Scotland and Ireland. In England, popular support for parliament greatly increased after the failed coup in January 1642, which also strengthened the parliamentary leadership's determination to press ahead with its radical reform programme. The propaganda war began and as commands were met with counter-commands, armed conflict at local level and involving all classes escalated. However reluctant the participants, they were soon lined up in a civil war which would affect many parts of the multiple kingdom.

Causes of the Frondes in France

Relative to the British Isles, France was a much bigger country and had a larger population. Its monarchy, like that of the multiple kingdom, was much troubled by domestic and external troubles, exacerbated by economic problems and a degree of social unrest. So how did the circumstances underpinning the Frondes in France compare with those in the British Isles? If there are direct comparisons we ought to be able to apply roughly the same model sketched out above.

Exercise   From reading Briggs, pp.105–22 what factors can you identify as promoting instability in the years before 1648? Note that you may also need to refer to earlier sections of Briggs. A few points have already been mentioned above to get you started. Try to see the relationships between the various factors as you write them down.

Discussion   This provides a summary of the main points you ought to have picked out – though it's by no means an exhaustive list.

Economic	Political
General economic recession	Hostility to innovations of central power
Subsistence crises	Hostility to Richelieu's supporters and his use of patronage to maintain and extend his influence
Increasing tax demands	Rivalries and disagreements within the royal family
Depredations of troops	Noble conspiracies 1626–32 and 1641–2
	Problems associated with an administration run by venal office-holders
	Feelings among many that ancient rights were under attack

You might say that some factors are not easily placed in one category or another, for example the attacks by the rural poor on the towns because of a perception that it was townsfolk who were responsible for rising tax demands, and there were tax revolts in the towns too.

Undoubtedly there are some interesting points of comparison between the situation in France and that in England. There was a similar atmosphere of economic uncertainty mainly caused by harvest failures and agricultural depression which affected all classes of society, increasing resentment of royal authority, innovation, patronage and privilege; opposition to taxation and particularly that directed at the promotion of war; social tensions seen in the popular revolts which preceded the Frondes themselves. A growth in the urban population was bringing similar social and economic problems to French towns and cities to those we noted above in England, particularly London.

Economically, many of the problems before the Frondes arose from the fact that the price of grain was stagnating rather than rising (see Briggs, Graph 1). The bulk of the population, peasant farmers, was being taxed more heavily at a time when its income was static. The problem was all the more acute in that many seigneurs were also feeling the pinch from lack of expansion of their income from the land and thus was leading them to increase pressure on their peasants, who were thus doubly pressed. Against this backdrop, the sudden rise in prices in the late 1640s could have been very positive because it might have allowed greater profits for farmers. But, in fact, the price rise was caused by very bad harvests, which meant that proportionately fewer peasants had any surplus to market at all. So the problem was doubled.

While the level of social ferment experienced in the city of Bordeaux in the 1630s and 1640s was perhaps greater than in other places, the fundamental problems were the same. Citizens of all classes had to contend with a sharp rise in prices. Between 1635 and 1648 the price of wheat rose by 60 per cent, that of beef by 20 per cent, that of mutton by 25 per cent, and wine by 30 per cent. The increases were partly the result of natural calamities, such as hail, the principal enemy of the vine, and floods which destroyed much of the cereal and vegetable crops. Apart from price rises, an equally significant factor was the unsound coinage. France was being flooded with inferior foreign coins and the presence of such coins, coupled with the practice of coin clipping, had so reduced their worth, that in 1643 one of these coins, the *dénier double*, was devalued by 50 per cent. Intended as a monetary reform, and as a means of increasing the government's revenues, this action hit ordinary folk badly. The *doubles* had 'so filled the province that no other coins are to be found among the common people'. Not only had their debts doubled, but they also found that no one would take the coins. 'The wheat merchants', the *Jurade* (municipal authority) reported, 'are refusing to accept the *Deniers* and this has caused murmuring among the common people who are in possession of this money'. The resistance was apparently so great that the Bordeaux *parlement* had to issue a decree ordering 'all persons to accept the *doubles* ... on pain of exemplary punishment' (Westrich, 1972, pp.8–12).

These were difficult years for the citizens of Bordeaux, particularly the lower classes who were forced to bear the brunt of royal taxation. Their response, as Westrich has indicated, was to rise in revolt, first against the government's fiscal agents, then against the municipal authorities, and finally against the government itself. A series of disturbances preceded the first major insurrection of May–June 1635, which came in response to a new wine tax. Crowds took to the streets, two tax collectors were massacred and the homes of others pillaged and burnt; the *Hotel de Ville* (Town Hall) was seized, with its records torched; the gaol emptied; a priest burnt alive; and a number of soldiers shot. The insurrection ended but only after the Duke of Épernon had entered the city at the head of an army and killed more than a score of rebels.

Subsequent disturbances in Bordeaux were also primarily economic in origin. In 1636 riots broke out over the export of grain and many bourgeois and other inhabitants refused to take up arms to support a militia half-weakened by plague. Other disorders, precipitated by shortages and near-famine, occurred in 1638, 1642 and 1643. The last initially focused on a ship laden with grain for export, which caused a 'general upheaval', since at that time wheat was triple its normal price. Again, the bourgeois and merchants, probably fearing further attacks on their property, refused to support the authorities, who had little choice but to heed the insurgents' demand and allow the vessel to be unloaded. This marked a turning point in the relationship between the various classes and interest groups, for the Bordeaux *parlement* became the adjudicator in disputes and then the effective ally of the lower classes. According to Westrich, the ground had been laid for the first Fronde 'when *Parlement* and "menu" people would close ranks to fight their common enemy'. The Bordeaux *parlement* and the lower classes seemed to be lining up against the bourgeois and the merchants, but the prime enemy was the royal government. The idea of local élites allying with the lower orders is fundamental to the pre-Frondes disputes. At stake was:

1   the wish for local élites to have first pick of the peasant surplus;

2   the wish of local élites to keep order and maintain local liberties.

Class questions broke down the alliance when things got out of hand. Bordeaux may have been the most radical and politically conscious place, but the pre-conditions were replicated in much the same form elsewhere in France during the run-up to the Frondes.

The Frondes were primarily backlashes against the 'administrative revolution' and the new institutions of absolutism. As Briggs shows (pp.118–22) the administrative reforms were mainly aimed at improving the efficiency of revenue collection for the crown. However, the crown failed to reorganize the underlying institutions, and the financial administrators, by resorting to malpractice, managed to obscure the picture of what happened in royal finances. In its search for short-term credit the crown operated outside the law, reconciling its actions by means of devices like forged documents which would satisfy the vigilance of bodies like the *Chambre des Comptes* and hopefully allay the suspicion of the population at large. The fictitious or fraudulent documents covered up the high interest rates the crown paid for credit, a price far above the legal interest rate of 5.5 per cent. There was corruption at the highest level. The crown, desperate for funds, sought loans from anyone with money in return for a great range of privileges and favours, to prop up its creaking finances.

At that point there was little active conflict between Catholics and Protestants on confessional grounds. Protestants who held royal offices seem to have been more concerned with their privileges as office-holders than as Protestants. A greater force towards instability was the feeling, held deeply by the king and his ministers, that Huguenots could not be loyal subjects of the crown because their religion divided their loyalties from the king. For the central decades of the seventeenth century Protestantism was not the political issue it had been earlier – and would be later.

More specifically, the power, wealth and patronage of Richelieu, Mazarin and other senior churchmen was both resented and feared by those nobles at court or in the country who had not been favoured as office-holders by these and other powerful ministers. Already they felt themselves under financial pressure and perhaps even cheated, and worse was to come.

According to Mettam (1988), ministerial responsibility for provoking unrest was considerable. Most of the Frondeurs, and especially the office-holders themselves, shared the royal desire for an orderly, well-administered country. It was only the exceptionally acute financial problems of the state as a result of involvement in the Thirty Years' War which led Mazarin to implement drastic financial policies, that would inevitably be challenged by local élites and even by the state's own bureaucrats, which caused them to take such dramatic action against the ruling regime. They were mainly concerned to resist attempts by Mazarin to undermine local, social and institutional privileges. So they scrutinized royal policies and resisted those they did not like. Mazarin himself was widely distrusted and as a foreign cleric was a hated figure. As an outsider he lacked family connections which might have enabled him to build up a network of patronage in order to counter those of princely nobles and office-holding opponents.

Fiscal policy in the form of provocative wartime taxes and financial expedients undoubtedly lay at the root of the crisis of 1648. We'll return to further points of comparison and contrast later. Now let's look at the crises themselves and the course of events in England, Ireland and France.

The course of the civil wars

The basis of your work in the following sections is an analysis of key events in the British Isles and France based on your reading in the set books. Let's start with the course of events in England and the implications for the other parts of the multiple kingdom.

Exercise   Read Coward, pp.204–36 and then answer the following questions:

1   Which main groups became embroiled in the conflicts and why do you think they did so?

2   Bearing in mind that this is one historian's interpretation of events, what do you think are the major difficulties between historians on this issue?

3   Looking specifically at pp.217–19, what do you think were the main effects of the war on English society?

Discussion   1   As you can see, the issue is undoubtedly complicated. As Coward makes clear, there weren't two easily identifiable sides: groupings and alignments changed in the course of the war. Some preferred to remain neutral – perhaps mindful of the horrors and devastation of the Thirty Years' War still raging in Europe. However, with many qualifications, the Royalist cause did appeal more to landowners and merchants, whilst lesser gentry, small farmers, small merchants and craftsmen looked to the Parliamentarian cause. Social and economic factors were important in determining which side individuals chose to support. It is nevertheless important to bear in mind that politics and religion played an important role, that there were great regional variations in support for one side or the other, and that initially neutralism played a larger part than activism.

However, the activists were soon to draw up the dividing lines. Many people found it difficult to commit themselves to one side or the other, but even the emergence of a strong neutralist movement could not halt the war.

2   The civil war is one of the most intensively researched periods of British history, but there are still many aspects of it about which we know little. In Unit 4 we will look at some of the issues which most concern historians of this period and observe that a lively debate continues around this subject. While there are divisions of opinion between historians with different ideological viewpoints, hypotheses are often made about the civil wars and those who participated 'without sufficient factual basis'. On this question, as with so many others surrounding these complex events, there appears to be no shortage of theories about who participated in the English Revolution. The crux of the issue is why did individuals irrespective of their social status or wealth, take the stance that they did? Were people genuinely divided? What about those who remained strictly neutral?

3   The wars affected, in one way or another, all sections of the population and no-one's life was untouched by them. Taxation was increased as a direct outcome of the war and troops were billeted on civilians with little recompense. Looting and pillage were common and for the civilian population caught up in a war area there was constant disruption to daily life.

At another level, it is obvious that the economies of towns and villages in areas affected by the war suffered. Anti-war feeling emerged, but it was not until 1645 that there is evidence of resistance to the armies of both sides. The Clubmen movement was essentially a protest against the disruption caused by the two opposing factions.

There was certainly a strong popular level of participation, even if there hadn't been much enthusiasm about going to war in the first place. People felt they lived in extraordinary times, that the world had been turned upside down, that Christ's second coming was just round the corner, that divine providence was directing their lives and that the prophesies of the Bible were being acted out. In the midst of economic disruption, conscription, epidemics, political and religious turmoil, there were many deaths. People died for what they believed in.

Reading a portrait: visual evidence of the taking of sides

For this section you will need the Illustration Book (Col.Pls 5–7). It will take you about 30 minutes.

We have seen how the English civil war affected all sections of society, but whilst the whole country was divided over matters of fundamental importance, participants in the two sides of the war did not cease to share a common culture and people's social aspirations did not change. Nobles on each side expected to be treated as nobles, deference was not abolished. In this section of the unit, we shall look at how this common culture was manifested in portraiture. We shall look at how a historian can use portraits as evidence for the seventeenth century. You will start with looking at a portrait of the Earl of Strafford in the Illustration Book and trying to answer some questions about it, the discussion follows on video 3. There is a discussion then of a further portrait, of Venetia Stanley, on the video and exercises on portraits of Henrietta Maria and Sir Edward Massey.

Video Exercise 1   Look at the Illustration Book, Col. Pl. 5 and try to answer the following questions:

    1   What sort of person is being portrayed?

    2   Of what status?

    3   What does the background show?

    4   What objects are to be seen and where are they in relation to the subject?

    5   Is there any indication *on the canvas* as to who the subject is (writing, coats of arms etc.)?

Discussion   Now watch Part 1 of video 3 for the discussion and continue with Part 2 for the discussion of a further portrait.

Now return to the Illustration Book, Col. Pl. 6.

Video Exercise 2   Setting yourself the same questions as we asked above, what do you make of this portrait?

Discussion   Watch Part 3 of the video for a discussion of the portrait of Henrietta Maria.

Video Exercise 3   Now ask yourself the same questions of the portrait shown in the Illustration Book, Col. Pl. 7.

Discussion   1   The portrait of Sir Edward Massey (*c.*1619–*c.*1674) shows a young gentleman in military clothing (buff coat, breast-plate and sword), the clothing of an active soldier, but also holding a cane, a civilian accoutrement.

    2   His sword and clothing indicate a man of some status, as does the style of the portrait, which is in a similar genre to that of Strafford.

    3   The background shows a battle scene, further suggesting that the subject was an active soldier, though the subject himself is shown withdrawn from the battle in a rustic setting.

    4   The objects, the helmet and the foliage, further suggest a soldier, but one who is slightly disengaged.

    5   There is no inscription on the picture to tell us who the subject is.

As you can see, there are similarities between this portrait and the portrait of Strafford. This is a portrait in the court style, painted by Peter Lely probably in 1647 or 1648, one of his earliest non-royal, full-length portraits. But how do we know who the subject is? The Van Dyck portraits we have already looked at are well documented and the appearance of two of the sitters is, in any case, well known. Both Wentworth and the queen were often painted. As we have noted, there is nothing on the picture to say who the man is and, in the absence of documents from Lely's studio or of a long provenance (the history of its ownership), the identity of the sitter may be uncertain.

As you may see from the captions, the subject is Sir Edward Massey, a *parliamentarian* general, commander of the Western army and defender of the city of Gloucester during a month-long siege in 1643. It was probably painted shortly after he fell out with the high command of the New Model Army and sided with the Presbyterians (see Coward, p.229). Thus it shows a military man of action, but one who has actually withdrawn from the fray (indicated by the juxtaposition of the military accoutrements with the cane and the separation of Massey from the battle scene). The sitter has been identified as Massey since the nineteenth century. Assuming that this identification is correct, what makes this portrait so interesting is that here is a parliamentarian gentleman being depicted in a very similar way to prominent royalists. This picture reflects his valour and status, not his politics.

Ireland

In religion, politics, administration and culture Ireland, like Scotland, was quite different from England. At the beginning of the seventeenth century, following the accession of James I to the throne of England which also made him king of Scotland, Irish history entered an important new phase. The Irish historian Aidan Clark has summed up the history of Ireland in the first half of the seventeenth century as 'rich in event and perhaps bewildering in the number and complexity of the interests involved. The Irish, the Old English, the New English, the royalists, the parliamentarians and the Scots – each of them played their separate parts in the confusion of events. But what happened at that time can be summarised in a single brief sentence. The land of Ireland changed hands' (Clark, 1967, p.189).

In Ireland the native chiefs, though no longer politically independent, still retained large tracts of land, albeit under English law. The Old English, the descendants of the Anglo-Norman settlers, had a dominant position among the nobility and gentry of Leinster and Munster and in the towns. Both Irish and Old English were predominantly Catholic and they formed the land-owning and trading classes.

However, there was a growing English, chiefly Protestant, population. This group mainly comprised soldiers, government officials, and investors, many of whom had recently become landowners. It was crown policy to promote the interests of this group through the encouragement of 'plantation' or land settlement, particularly in Ulster. The policy of plantation was given a strong boost by the 'Flight of the Earls', the two earls Tyrone and Tyrconnel. Quitting Ireland with their followers in 1607, their estates and those of their followers were confiscated and large areas of the province of Ulster were settled by Protestants, both English and Scots (see Fig. 20). There was no large-scale removal of the native Irish

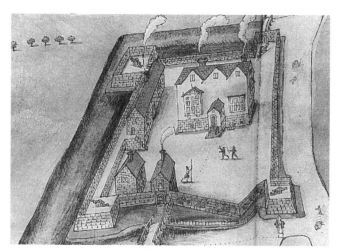

Figure 19
House and fort at Omagh, *detail from seventeenth-century map,*
Trinity College Library Dublin TCD MS 1209/33. Reproduced by
permission of the Board of Trinity College, Dublin.

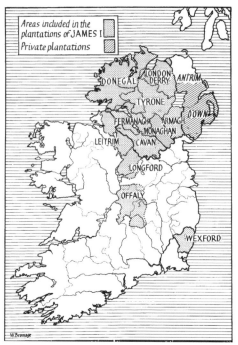

Figure 20
Plantations of James I, *from Ruth Dudley Edwards,* An atlas of
Irish History, *1973, reproduced by permission of Routledge.*

and the progress of the plantation was slow, but it gradually built up
momentum, and by 1628 it is estimated there were 2,000 English and
Scots families settled in the 'planted' counties. The slow but relentless
spread of the plantations was to have a profound effect on the political
and religious life of Ulster, which proved to be a crucial theatre in the
events leading to the insurrection of 1641.

Whilst the Old English were not directly affected by the Ulster confiscations and plantations, they were at odds with James I's policies and
those of his son. Their grievance was a religious one and they viewed the
frequent proclamations against Catholics with growing alarm and hostility. The government feared a political alliance between the co-religionists,
the Irish and the Old English, though their fear almost certainly had little
foundation. Much of the unrest in Ireland, then, centred around land
and religion.

Charles I, as part of his policy to raise revenue, struck a deal with
the Irish landowners. In return for certain concessions, financial help
would be forthcoming. Under this scheme landowners were given special
guarantees and in some cases the Oath of Supremacy was relaxed. An
Irish parliament was to approve these royal concessions – known as 'the
Graces', but the parliament never met and 'the Graces' came to depend
solely on the king's pleasure. The activities of the Jesuits in Ireland gave
cause of alarm but various attempts at suppression angered Catholics.

Ireland appeared to be becoming less and less governable. As we
saw in Unit 2, Charles appointed as Lord Deputy, Sir Thomas Wentworth,
who ruled Ireland with a strong hand from 1633 to 1640. His policy was
to use Ireland's resources to strengthen the monarchy and to destroy any
group or institution which opposed the absolute authority of the crown.

Royal power was to remain in England, and Ireland was to be transformed into a dependent state. For example, the woollen industry was not allowed to develop so that Ireland became increasingly dependent on England for supplies, for as Wentworth wrote, 'All wisdom advises to keep this kingdom as much subordinate and dependent on England as is possible; and holding them for the manufacture of wool, and thus enforcing them to fetch their clothing from thence... How can they depart from us without nakedness and beggary' (quoted in Beckett, 1979, p.68).

These policies caused great resentment and contributed to the outbreak of rebellion in 1641. This insurrection while undoubtedly of great consequence, has become enshrouded in many of the myths which have plagued Irish history, for as Foster (1988, p.86) writes 'what people thought happened in that bloody autumn conditioned attitudes in Ireland for generations to come'. He further observes that 'those who led the revolt were not the dispossessed natives, driven beyond endurance; nor were they the fanatically Catholic revanchists. They were the Ulster gentry, of Irish origin, but still "the deserving Irish" whose interests had survived the plantations'. Throughout Ulster the native Irish rose up against the colonists and planters. Historians remain divided as to the exact aims of the rebels since the rebels were loud in the affirmations of loyalty to the crown. In fact, Sir Phelim O'Neill, as leader of the insurgents, maintained that he was acting upon the direct orders of the king.

What does seem clear in this confused situation is that the Old English, especially those who lived outside the former Pale (the area around Dublin), had fewer grievances than the native Irish of Ulster. Their natural tendency was to support the crown, but they were linked by religion to the native Irish. They were undoubtedly concerned – like their Ulster co-religionists – with the views increasingly expressed in the Long Parliament, which was beginning to take a strongly Protestant line. As Coward indicates (pp.199–200) much of the history of the rebellion remains obscure, but many colonists were driven from their lands and died during the fighting. It's important to note that the rebellion was against all the new settlements in Ireland but because the greatest number were in Ulster it bore the brunt of attacks. Such episodes as the attack by Catholics on Protestants at Portadown have become legendary. In November 1641 Protestants trying to cross the river were thrown off the bridge into the river. Those who did not drown were killed as they tried to swim ashore. Elizabeth Prize of Armagh managed to survive after her five children were pushed from the Portadown Bridge and gave evidence to the later enquiry into Protestants' losses:

> And as for this deponent and many others that were stayed behind, diverse tortures were used upon them ... and this deponent for her part was thrice hanged up to confess to money, and afterwards let down, and had the soles of her feet fried and burnt at the fire and was often scourged and whipt ...
>
> And a great number of other Protestants, principally women and children, whom the rebels would take, they pricked and stabbed with their pitchforks, skeans and swords and would slash, mangle and cut them in their heads and breasts, faces, arms and hands and other parts of their bodies, but not kill them outright but leave them wallowing in their blood to languish and starve them to death. (Quoted in Kee, 1980, p.43)

It is difficult to know what reliance to put on such a testimony made some time after the event. However, there is much evidence to show that the incident at Portadown took place and it is clear that other massacres also occurred.

Some estimates give the number killed being as high as 200,000 but this seems very exaggerated. Modern historians would now place the number at 4,000 with retaliatory attacks against Catholics accounting for almost as many deaths. Nevertheless, the horror stories spread, and in both Dublin and London calls for reprisals against all Catholics irrespective of race were vociferous. It was therefore inevitable that the Old English soon joined the insurgents. This led to combined forces laying siege to Drogheda in 1641 and a general invasion of the Pale and the spread of the fighting to Munster.

The situation in Ireland was made more acute by the outbreak in England of the civil war in August 1642. The insurgents set up a central government at Kilkenny under the direction of the Catholic bishops. The Confederation of Kilkenny, as it was known, though in armed dispute against the government, nevertheless stressed its continuing loyalty to the crown. In the Protestant camp there was just as much confusion. While there was universal fear of the rebels and what they represented, there were also those who thoroughly distrusted the king and those who supported parliament. What is clear is that the attitude of every group, whether Catholic or Protestant, was shaped by the land question. The native Irish, especially those in Ulster, had little landed property. They looked for the complete restoration of their confiscated lands and to this extent were more 'hard line' than their Old English allies, who still possessed their estates. The Protestants were, in the main, anxious to suppress the rebels, whether native Irish or Old English, and acquire more land.

Figure 21
The Siege of Drogheda, *woodcut. British Museum Dept. of Prints and Drawings, reproduced by permission of the Trustees.*

Exercise   Examine *Anthology* I.14 and I.15 and compare and contrast the demands by the Catholic Confederacy and by the Protestants to Charles I in April 1644. What are the Catholics asking for and what are the Protestants asking for? In what way are their demands completely at odds with one another?

Discussion   Catholic claims are for a redress of grievances and guarantees against confiscation of land but they are essentially looking for a return to the situation which they enjoyed before the appointment of Wentworth. Further they wish to be exonerated of the crimes of 1641 and that they retain their religious freedom. The Protestant claims are quite unequivocal. Existing restraints on Catholics should be continued and, as far as the Catholic clergy are concerned, extended. Clearly they are at odds with each other both on religious and economic grounds.

Figure 22
Settlers houses and
church, County Derry, *from
Map of the Fishmongers at
Ballykelly in the Survey by
Thomas Phillips and Ralph
Hudson, 1622. National
Library of Ireland.*

The English sent forces to Ireland during the 1640s, but it was not until 1649 that they were able to turn their attention fully to settling the war there. In that year Oliver Cromwell arrived with an army to subdue the Catholic rebels, a process which took until 1653 to complete.

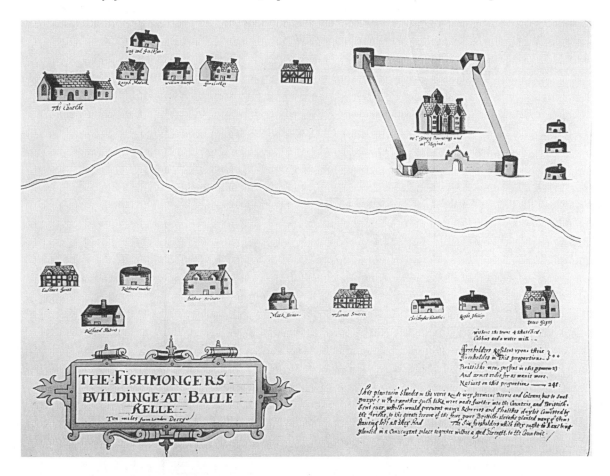

A dramatic change in the ownership of land had already occurred. In 1603 much of the cultivable land in each of the four provinces was still held by Catholics. Around 1641 it is estimated that the proportion of land owned by Catholics had been reduced to slightly under two-thirds. Plantations and seizures accounted for the great bulk of this transfer, exclusively to Protestants. In the aftermath of the civil wars Ireland was dealt with ruthlessly by Cromwell and as Clark (1967) observed, this suppression was mainly targeted at those who had been involved in the rebellion:

> It was the wealth of the land of Ireland that the government of England was interested in. And it reserved its special fury for those who owned that land. It divided landholders in Ireland into two groups – those who had been guilty of involvement in the rebellion, and those who had not. The first were to lose all their estates, and all their property rights. The second were to be allowed to own a proportion of the amount of land which they had held. But it was not to be the same land. Ireland, also was to be divided into two parts. The first part was to consist of Connaught and Clare, to which all who had established their innocence were to be transplanted and in which they were to receive the land to which they were entitled. The second part was to be the remaining twenty-six counties, which were to become the property of the government. In the main, this land was used to pay the government's creditors – the adventurers who had lent money or provided supplies for the army, and the officers and soldiers who had served without adequate pay. (Clark, 1967, pp.202–3)

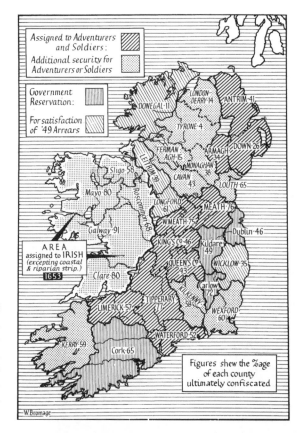

Figure 23
Cromwellian and Restoration land confiscations 1653–5, from Ruth Dudley Edwards, An atlas of Irish History, 1973, reproduced by permission of Routledge.

Though many of the ordinary soldiers did settle on the small pieces of land which they were given, many others sold out their interest and returned to England. The ones who did remain were the officers and adventurers who had received substantial grants. In fact, the arrangements made for the settlement of Irish land under Cromwell never approached the thoroughness intended by those who had planned the earlier plantation in Ulster. No organized attempt was made to establish Protestant communities, except in the towns. What was changed was the people who owned the land, not the people who lived and worked upon it. The Cromwellian settlement was not so much a plantation, as a transference of the sources of wealth and power from Catholics to Protestants. What it created was not a Protestant community, but a Protestant upper class. The newcomers managed to hold on to a great deal of what they had gained. And just as James I's plantation had permanently altered the character of Ulster, so Cromwell's settlement transformed the character of the land-owning aristocracy of Ireland.

By 1660, Catholics whatever their origin, were allowed to own land only to the west of the River Shannon in the province of Connaught and their share of the country rapidly declined. By 1688 it had fallen below a quarter of the land area.

Exercise   Now listen to the AC1, section 2, to see how the English understood the rebellion in Ireland.

The Frondes

We've already addressed some of the underlying causes so we can now consider the events themselves.

Exercise   Read Briggs, pp.126–34, picking out the key developments. Then in a short paragraph summarize what the wars of the Frondes were all about.

Discussion   Your answer should be something along these lines, but don't worry if you have not got every detail exactly right.

The Frondes were a series of civil wars which took place in France from 1648 to 1652 when France came under the rule of the regent, Anne of Austria and Mazarin during the minority of King Louis XIV. While the causes of the Frondes, were very complex, the disturbances can be regarded essentially as tax revolts. The insurrections took the form of large-scale urban riots, peasant revolts in the countryside, with ructions at court, various attempted *coups d'état*. There were two principal series of revolts – the Fronde of the *parlements* and the Fronde of the nobles.

Let's look at the events of the two Frondes in a bit more detail now.

The Fronde of the parlements

During the early months of 1648 the government put intensive pressure on the *parlement* of Paris to accept some of the new taxes but met with a strong refusal to pay. Attempts to extend long-standing taxes such as the *paulette* (see Briggs, pp.78–80) created an upsurge in unity among royal officials and opposition to further taxation. The *Chambre Saint Louis* (a joint assembly of the four sovereign courts of Paris – see Briggs, pp.126–7) adopted a declaration on 2 July 1648 by which the *parlement* was to have complete control of taxation. The *taille* was to be reduced by one-quarter and taxes were to be assessed and collected by local officials not by the *intendants* (the royal agents sent into the provinces). Further, a *Chambre de Justice* was to be established which would investigate the affairs of the financiers. *Lettres de Cachet* were to be abolished and a system of habeas corpus was to be introduced in order that all those arrested come to trial within twenty-four hours. On these and other measures the *Chambre Saint Louis* had the backing of the provincial *parlements*. At first Mazarin made some minor concessions but encouraged by the news of the Prince de Condé's great victory at Lens he went on the attack. Three leaders of the Paris *parlement*, including the popular Pierre Broussel, were arrested – an event which gave rise to several days of rioting in Paris. Mazarin was forced to release Broussel and the court had to flee Paris. The two sides eventually reached a compromise through the Treaty of Rueil in March 1649, which acknowledged the acceptance by the crown of the programme drawn up by the *Chambre Saint Louis*. Yet this could not provide the basis for a stable settlement. The crown was hobbled in its efforts to centralize power and to continue to engage in war, for although France had concluded its war in Germany (the Thirty Years' War) in 1648, war continued with Spain until 1659. Mazarin and Anne of Austria were soon doing their utmost to withdraw the programme of concessions. On the other hand, the Rueil agreement had failed to offer adequate compensation and rewards to the highest nobility who resented Mazarin's continuing hold on power, and intrigued against the Cardinal Minister and among themselves to secure political dominance on the royal council.

The Fronde of the nobles

The Fronde of the nobles – spanning the years 1650–3 – took place in both Paris and the provinces but especially in Bordeaux. Alliances were constantly formed and reformed among the major protagonists: Mazarin and the Queen Regent, who maintained a seemingly solid alliance; the *parlement*, most of whose members continued to demand the implementation of the *Chambre Saint Louis* programme; and an assortment of high nobles seeking political rewards and a hold on power. The mightiest of the noble Frondeurs, the Prince de Condé, defeated royal troops led by Turenne to capture Paris in July 1652. He played his hand badly. He turned against the Paris *parlement*, flirted with radical elements within Paris, and allied with the Spanish in the Netherlands. He lost much support among the social élite, and his position was further weakened by the proclamation of the young Louis XIV, and then by the decision of Mazarin to go into exile. Condé carried on the fight in Bordeaux, linking up with the Ormée movement – perhaps the most radical movement of the Fronde, which had a republican tinge to it. Some of the Ormée rebels looked to England for help, but this never materialized. The Ormée collapsed and with the royal forces gradually re-establishing order throughout France, Condé went into exile, thus ending the Fronde.

You can obtain a more detailed picture of these complex events from Briggs, using his glossary and index for explanations of French terms.

Exercise   Now read *Anthology*, I.15—17, then answer the following questions:

1   With reference to *Anthology*, I.15 how serious were the events of August 1648 detailed by Wicquefort?

2   What does the short extract in *Anthology*, I.16 tell us about the situation in Bordeaux?

3   What does *Anthology*, I.17 suggest about the 'English connection' with Bordeaux and the Ormée?

Discussion   1   It is clear that serious rioting took place in Paris. A royal official was attacked and troops killed. Barricades were erected by the rioters. These events can be seen as a serious challenge to royal authority. The arrest of Broussel and Blancmesnil, two of the opposition leaders, provoked further unrest. By its mishandling of the situation the Regency government managed to unite different social groups and in face of such a concerted front had no option but to release the two opposition leaders.

2   It would seem that the richer citizens of Bordeaux gathered regularly to discuss the high level of taxation and more general political issues of the day. These meetings aroused the interest and curiosity of the general public, who were also concerned about levels of taxation. Debate was lively and prolonged. Ultimately the assemblies were outlawed by the *parlement*.

3   The 'English connection', as far as Bordeaux was concerned, was an important one because of the wine trade.

Obviously there was wide knowledge of the chain of events in England and it seems there was talk of having a more representative parliament.

The Ormée of Bordeaux was more radical than other elements in the Fronde, but, as Bonney (Offprint 4) makes clear in your comparative reading, the label 'republican' was more a term of abuse than an accurate description used by political opponents. Even in England those holding republican views were an uninfluential minority: for Bonney the execution of the king could be seen as an act of political necessity. While there were protests about greater representation in Bordeaux they were scarcely republican in character.

For their part, the leaders of the Ormée were anxious to cultivate Condé and he reciprocated these feelings, as he made clear in the following letter to them:

> The letter in which you assure me of your good will could not have touched me more deeply... I am confident that the sentiments you express will persist to the very end, as they accord perfectly with your best interests. For had my enemies succeeded in my capture, the return of Cardinal Mazarin would have surely followed, with consequences that you would have been the first to feel ... Be assured that I shall remain steadfast in my resolve not to tolerate the return of the Cardinal or any of his creatures. (Bourdeaux, 1651)

Historians place various interpretations on the Frondes, which were certainly inspired by ill-feeling about the extension of royal authority and innovation, particularly with regard to fiscal policy and taxation, much as in England and Scotland. Bonney thinks that there is little similarity between the civil war in England and the wars of the Frondes in France. The revolutionary experience in England was totally different since at no time did the French contemplate getting rid of their monarchy. Also there were many elements of conservative reaction in the Frondes.

The Frondes failed in their principal objective, namely to check the administrative centralization of the French monarchy, and the growth of absolutism. Historians do now contend, however, that Frondeur resistance did restrain the full impact of the policies sketched out by Richelieu and Mazarin. Louis XIV's absolutism was arguably less absolute in practice than it made itself appear in theory and propaganda. Fear of another Fronde checked absolutist ambitions, and helped to influence the emergence of a delicate but lasting balance between monarchy, government and vested interests.

'A revolution ... and a relatively small revolution'

Thus the historian, Trevor–Roper, described the English civil war and the Frondes. Was he right? We can now make a more detailed comparison of the two conflicts. To help you do so read Offprint 4 and note the main points of comparison and contrast highlighted there.

Exercise On the basis of your reading of Bonney (Offprint 4, from the beginning of Section II) make a list showing the key comparisons and contrasts between the two civil wars.

Discussion While you may not have picked up all these points, and they are not necessarily in any rank order, your list should look something like this.

Comparisons

Both countries were monarchies, Charles attempting to model his regime on that of France.

The events were both triggered by crises at home and abroad (e.g. the Thirty Years' War; rebellion in Scotland and Ireland; tax revolt in France; Spanish intervention).

Crises of royal finance were common to both contexts. Increased taxation – partly caused by strategic needs – was the key factor in both instances. It affected most classes (but not the French nobility).

Normal government was either disrupted or suspended in both countries.

Arrest or attempted arrest of parliamentary leaders in England and of *parlementaires* in France.

Both civil wars were by no means exclusively metropolitan in character and involved the participation of many groups in both societies.

National rebellion in Ireland/Scotland and regional rebellion in France played important roles in triggering events.

There was strong multi-national participation in England, Scotland and Ireland and regional participation in France.

External influences were common to both conflicts – the Scots in England and the Spanish in France.

Contrasts

The English civil war was a revolution against the king and the way he exercised his powers by those outside the court whereas the Frondes were dominated by office-holders and nobles. Note, though, that all ranks of society were involved.

Religion was a major factor in the British Isles but not in France – though note that it was of some influence in the aftermath of the Frondes.

Royal revenue was substantially higher (five times) in France than in England.

Parliamentary government, although restricted, was more developed in England, Ireland and Scotland than in France.

English local administration was uniformly organized throughout the country and relied on unpaid members of the gentry. French local administration relied on a combination of royal officials and semi-independent noblemen as provincial governors.

The English civil wars probably involved more participants than the Frondes. Both events were widespread geographically with few English counties unaffected by war – though the Midland counties, especially around Oxford, were most affected. In France, strife concentrated around Paris and the key provincial centres.

Fighting was less prolonged in France than in England.

The French Regency had a much stronger army than Charles could command in England, Scotland and Ireland.

There was less clearly organized popular participation in France than in England, where various popular movements, such as the Levellers, played a significant role.

If we stuck solely to this list we could reasonably conclude that there are as many points of comparison as contrast, but that of course would be simplistic and not entirely in line with Bonney's argument. Undoubtedly the contexts in which both events occurred were similar, particularly in regard to fiscal grievances, social and political tensions. Religion, while highly significant throughout the British Isles, hardly figured at all in France. Apart from Ireland, England and Wales and Scotland were mainly Protestant, though, as we saw Catholicism was still a big issue in much that happened in the 1640s. Since France was overwhelmingly Catholic, though with a small Protestant minority which had been and remained the object of periodic persecution, the issue hardly arose.

It's clear that on several counts – particularly the level of participation and widespread nature of the conflict – that the Frondes seemed to those in authority to be just as revolutionary as the English civil war. Although led in the early stages by elements of the administration, reacting against royal innovations, the Frondes were less likely to succeed because of their ill-defined aims and the strength of the French monarchy which had built up a powerful army and could count on the support of office-holders whose interests would be best served by a return to order.

Conclusion

The immediate outcome of the civil wars in the British Isles and the internal strife associated with the Frondes in France were quite different. In England they led ultimately to the major crisis of 1648–9, when in December parliament was purged, followed in January by the trial and execution of the king. This instituted the English Republic and the Cromwellian regime which, as we saw above, moved quickly to consolidate its position in the rest of the multiple kingdom by suppressing the rebellion in Ireland and then dealing with the troublesome Scots. As Coward observes, the Protectorate was not a revolutionary regime, but it had nevertheless achieved revolutionary objectives, which by comparison, was hardly a consequence of the Frondes. According to Briggs (p.133) the Frondes cannot really be described as a 'failed' revolution since it never really developed 'revolutionary' aims and was essentially a reaction against royal innovations. It failed as a check on royal authority – a marked contrast to the more dramatic outcome across the Channel.

References

Beckett, J. C. (1979), *A Short History of Ireland*, 6th edn, Hutchinson, London.

Bourdeaux (1651), *Lettre de monseignuer le prince de Condé, gouverneur de Guyenne à messieurs les bourgeois de l'Ormée de Bourdeaux.*

Clark, A. (1967), 'The Colonisation of Ulster and the Rebellion of 1641' in T. W. Moody and F. X. Martin (eds), *The Course of Irish History*, Mercier Press.

Dent, J. (1973), *Crisis in Finance: Crown, Financiers and Society in Seventeenth Century France*, David & Charles, Newton Abbot.

Foster, R.F. (1988), *Modern Ireland, 1600–1972*, Allen Lane and The Penguin Press, London.

Gardiner, S.R. (1906), *Constitutional Documents of the Puritan Revolution*, Oxford University Press, Oxford.

Kee, R. (1980), *Ireland: A History*, Weidenfeld and Nicolson, London.

Mandrou, R. (ed.) (1978), *Abraham de Wicquefort. Chronique Discontinue de la Fronde 1648–1652*, Librairie Fayard, Paris.

Mettam, R. (1988), *Power and Faction in Louis XIV's France*, Blackwell, Oxford.

Westrich, S.A. (1972), *The Ormée of Bordeaux. A Revolution During the Fronde*, Johns Hopkins University Press, Baltimore.

Unit 4
The causes of instability in England, Scotland, Ireland and France

Prepared for the course team by
Anne Laurence

Contents

Study timetable

Weeks of study	Texts	Video	AC	Set books
2	Illustration Book, *Anthology*, I.19, 20, Offprints 5,6,7	4		Coward, Briggs

During the period of this unit you should also watch TV5 and 6.

Objectives

At the end of this unit and on the basis of your knowledge of the causes and course of the civil wars in the British Isles and the Frondes in France from Units 2 and 3 you should understand:

1   why historians have different explanations for the civil wars and the Frondes;

2   how they reached these explanations.

You will also find material on French interpretations of the Fronde in the offprint, R. Knecht, *The Fronde.*

Introduction

In the units so far we have looked at the background and the course of the upheavals in France and the British Isles in the 1640s and 1650s. You will have noticed that the authors of the units refer to different interpretations of the events and their causes and to differences of approach between historians.

In this unit I want to look at some of these differences of approach and the reasons why historians ask different kinds of questions and come up with a variety of answers. This process is often dismissively described as historical fashion, but it is much more than that. It is by the constant interrogation of previous historians' work that we advance our knowledge. The historian of the English civil war, C.V. Wedgwood, wrote in 1955 that:

> The final, dispassionate, authoritative history of the Civil Wars cannot be written until the problems have ceased to matter: by that time it will not be worth writing. (quoted in Richardson, 1977, p.1)

I should perhaps add that C.V. Wedgwood is best known for providing a splendid narrative of the events of the civil war but without much explanation. But the point she makes is an important one. Civil wars, wars in which people take up arms against each other, are perhaps even more perplexing than wars between nations.

We shall start by looking at some of the types of explanation which historians of the seventeenth century have used, then at four specific explanations offered for the causes of the English civil war and the Frondes, and finally at two attempts to provide a single common explanation for the turmoils in mid-seventeenth-century Europe.

Types of explanation

In this section I shall look at some of the kinds of explanation which historians of the seventeenth century have advanced. Very broadly we may call these class, the economy, 'ins' and 'outs', and religion. I shall break these down further into social status, economic status, economic infrastructure, politics, and religion, ending with a section on 'revisionism'. But first I want to look at a set of terms which historians use extensively of this period and which, though apparently just descriptive, are actually much more loaded than they at first seem: civil war, revolt, rebellion and revolution.

Civil war, revolt, rebellion, and revolution

It is often said that one person's 'freedom fighter' is another person's 'rebel', and this is just as true of the seventeenth century as it is today, though the terminology is slightly different. We may learn a good deal about peoples' understanding of the civil wars of the seventeenth century

Figure 24
Oliver Cromwell, *from
Josiah Ricraft,* A Survey of
Englands Champions and
Truths faithfull Patriots,
1647.

by the terms they use. 'Civil war' is a fairly neutral term; often in seven-teenth-century English it was rendered as 'intestine war' (intestine mean-ing internal), 'unnatural war', or 'distractions'.

The term 'revolt' usually implies objections to authority of a fairly restricted kind. The refusal of many French people to pay taxes in the 1630s is often described as a 'tax revolt', though commonly violence broke out at the *perceived* threat of a new tax being levied rather than against an existing tax. We have already seen (Unit 1) how the citizens of Agen rioted in 1635 against the rumour that the *gabelle* (the tax on salt) was to be introduced. On another occasion the people of Thouars in Poitou cried: 'An agent is trying to bring in a new type of tax. We'll have to beat him up' (Bercé, 1990, p.227). Bercé, the historian of French popular revolts, argues that popular risings broke out all the time and were not regarded with hatred or fear by society at large. Popular revolts were not in them-selves very significant, they were manifestations of discontent by people who had no other form of expression; we might even see them as a form of collective bargaining. The authorities only became concerned when persons of influence, nobles, *parlementaires* and other royal officers were involved. England seems, by contrast, a very peaceable place. Refusal to pay ship money in the 1630s never amounted to a revolt, though the sher-iff of Dorset reported in 1636 that 'the greatest part of the arrears falls among the poorer sort who pay it like drops of blood' (Morrill, 1976, p.144). Occasionally, popular demonstrations took place against the enclosure of common land, the draining of fenland (turning common marshes into private farmland) or high grain prices. Lobbying parliament in the 1640s often produced demonstrations, as in November 1641:

> ... when many hundreds of citizens flocking to the houses of Parlia-ment, called earnestly upon the members as they passed by from their houses, to suppress bishops, crying aloud 'No bishops, no bishops', calling them limbs of Antichrist, which caused a great dis-pute what Antichrist was. (Proceedings, 1641, p.3)

But none of these really amounts to a revolt. The Prayer Book riots in Edinburgh in 1637 might have a better claim, but they rapidly escalated into a more organized form of resistance.

By contrast, 'rebellion' is a loaded term, carrying the implication that some person or body's lawful authority is being challenged. The Earl of Clarendon's magisterial history is entitled *The History of the Rebellion and Civil Wars in England*. He was a royalist and clearly saw the wars of the 1640s as rebellions, but was enough of a historian to recognize that the wars which took place in the 1650s were not rebellions, there being no lawfully constituted authority because the monarchy was in exile. The government of the Commonwealth, however, clearly regarded its opponents as rebels.

In July 1643 French Council of State issued a decree stating that:

> The populace are encouraged in the frequent rebellions which occur in the levy of the *taille* and subsistence [a military tax introduced in 1637 for the maintenance of the army during the winter] by the protection of the judges and magistrates ... [The king in his council] has declared and declares all those accused and convicted of sedition and public rebellion guilty of treason. (Bon-ney, 1988, p.219)

This shows very clearly how, in the eyes of the royal government, revolt was transformed into rebellion by the involvement of people of higher social status. The French government turned demonstrators into rebels by declaring their crime to be treason rather than breach of the peace.

But notice that this is occurring in 1643, two months into Anne of Austria's regency, not during the actual period of the Frondes, 1648–52, which we may certainly refer to as rebellions. A royal commissioner in the province of Guyenne, visiting Chancellor Séguier in July 1649, referred to the rebels there. But the government in 1649 was not in a position to assert itself against its opponents as unequivocally as it had in 1643.

The events of 1641 and later are commonly referred to as a 'rebellion' or 'rising' of the native Irish. The English press had no hesitation about referring to the 'rebellious papists' and their 'bloody and treasonable designs'. And the war was characterized as one about religion:

> These papists or rebels call it a religious war, ruin and desolation they threaten to the poor Protestants. (Ireland, 1641)

The English press, following proceedings in the English parliament, perceived the war as a rebellion by the Catholic Irish against the Protestant English, a point of view which was not informed by any knowledge of Ireland and its population. The Old English, Catholic descendants of the twelfth-century settlers, were far from wanting to throw in their lot with the Catholic Irish, not least because many of them occupied land confiscated from the Irish in the sixteenth and early seventeenth centuries. And for many of the Scots settlers in Ireland who had arrived in the early seventeenth century, the English government was associated with the attempt to impose an alien religious settlement on Scotland.

The First and Second Bishops' Wars of 1639 and 1640 can scarcely be called rebellions since they were invasions of England by a sovereign state (Scotland) which happened to share a monarch with England.

Governors used the term 'rebel' to justify their acting against people they perceived as opponents and to assert their own claims to legitimacy. People rarely referred to themselves as rebels, since to do so would have impugned the legitimacy of their protest.

A similarly slippery term is 'revolution', though unlike the term rebellion, it was not used in the seventeenth century in the sense of a total political, social, economic or religious upheaval, senses in which it is used by historians today. Just as the term 'rebellion' was used in the seventeenth century as a way of indicating the magnitude of a protest, the term 'revolution' is used by historians as a judgement of the scale of the upheaval. It is also used as a way of assessing the consequences of an episode rather than its causes, as we have seen in the discussion in Bonney's article (Offprint 4) and his quotation from Hugh Trevor-Roper in Unit 3.

Consider these quotations:

> … what was launched by the Ulster conspirators of 1641 was … nothing short of a revolution. (Canny, 1987, p.208)

> … when it dispersed on 20 December [1638] the [General] Assembly [of the kirk] had completed a religious revolution, but the political situation was precarious, and war was now inevitable. (Brown, 1992, p.116)

Notice how both writers use the term 'revolution' to make a judgement about the scale and impact of events early in the upheavals in Ireland and Scotland. But there are some differences in the way they use the term. For Canny the 'revolution' is synonymous with the spread of the Ulster rising to the rest of Ireland. For Brown the revolution was the degree of support for the National Covenant in the general assembly of the kirk and in parliament (where the majority of peers and members for the shires and all the members for the burghs voted for the Covenant and against episcopacy), the war with England was something separate.

You have seen from Unit 3 that historians of England have been in the habit of referring to the events there as a revolution, but there has not been unanimity about what constituted that revolution. Christopher Hill wrote an essay in 1940, 'The English Revolution 1640', and went on to write a book entitled *The Century of Revolution*.

Exercise   Please read Coward, pp.236–7. What does Coward identify as the English Revolution?

Discussion   Coward takes a narrowly political definition here (though notice that this whole section of the book, chapters 6 and 7, is titled 'The English Revolution 1640–1660'). The term revolution is being used to refer to the overthrow and abolition of the monarchy and the purge of parliament. It is a revolution, as he sees it, carried out without popular support but by a group of people outside the traditional ruling élite and with the backing of the parliamentary army. However, in the last sentence he does go on to suggest that the magnitude of the revolution was in fact rather greater.

Figure 25
Sir Thomas Fairfax, *from Josiah Ricraft*, A Survey of Englands Champions and Truths faithfull Patriots, *1647.*

The first writer to use the term 'revolution' of the English civil war in the sense in which we would recognize the term was the French historian François Guizot, who did so in 1826 when comparing the English revolution with the French revolution of 1789. 'Previous to the French revolution,' he wrote, the English revolution 'was the greatest event which Europe had to narrate … our revolution, in surpassing, did not make that of England less great in itself; they were both victories in the same war' (Guizot, 1890, p.ix). Guizot argued that there was nothing in either revolution which could not have been found already: 'they advanced civilization in the path it has been pursuing for fourteen centuries, the people supplanted the feudal aristocracy, the church and the monarchy in the possession of power' (Guizot, 1890, pp.xii–xv).

Might we term the Frondes a revolution? Roland Mousnier has referred to the days of barricades of 26–28 August 1648 as *journées révolutionnaires* (revolutionary days) which 'transformed a latent civil war into a situation of acute crisis' (Mousnier, 1977a, p.169). Members of the royal council decided to arrest those members of the Paris *parlement* who had been most vociferous in their objections to the court. They succeeded in arresting two of the most important *parlementaires*, whereupon the ordinary people of Paris – boatmen, artisans and beggars – rose to the defence of the imprisoned men. Respectable craftsmen and propertied people of the middling sort, fearful both of the rioters and of the soldiers sent to carry out the arrest, armed themselves. In the course of the next two days they made common cause with the *parlement* against the court and, early on 27 August, barricades were erected over much of Paris. Royal troops were sent out and leading members of the *parlement* went to the queen to demand the release of their imprisoned colleagues. The delegation, on its way back to discuss the terms offered them, was attacked by citizens who believed that they were being betrayed by the members of *parlement* who were now colluding with the court in a settlement which excluded their grievances. In the ensuing chaos no one knew what side anyone else was on. The revolutionary days came to an end on 28 August when everyone laid down their arms and the imprisoned *parlementaires* were released. This was an episode in the deterioration of relations between the court and the *parlementaires* which finally flared up into the *Fronde parlementaire* later in the year.

Bonney (Offprint 4, p.25) quotes Hugh Trevor-Roper's dictum that the Frondes constituted a 'relatively small revolution', but he also quotes Lloyd Moote (p.30), 'the Fronde was the most widespread of the rebellions in mid-seventeenth-century Europe' but concludes himself (p.30) that the 'revolutionary experience' in France was nothing like as intense as that in England. Certainly there were revolutionary moments in France, but it is difficult to see a single definable revolution in the events of the Frondes, nor, as we shall see in Unit 5, in their consequences.

As you can see, the term 'revolution' is used by historians in a number of different ways. It may refer to the scale or the scope of a conflict, or to its consequences, or to certain aspects of the conflict. But in all its uses of the upheavals of the mid-seventeenth century it gives us a sense of the different kinds of judgement being made by historians.

In the next five sections we shall look in more detail at some of the subjects upon which historians have concentrated in trying to explain the civil wars of the mid-seventeenth century. You have seen something of this in Unit 3, where you were introduced to some of the issues; here we shall concentrate upon how historians have used them.

Social status

Class is seen by many historians as one of the major engines of social change. As I mentioned in Unit 1, historians of the seventeenth century tend to prefer the term 'social status' to 'class', as class has overtones of class conflict and class relations in industrialized societies. In classical Marxist history the seventeenth century is seen as the period of bourgeois revolution when feudalism made way for capitalism, and when the economic infrastructure was transformed. This model has informed the study of the English civil war to a limited extent, but has had little impact on the history written of Ireland and Scotland in this period. However, it has informed a major debate on the history of France in the seventeenth century. In 1963 Professor Boris Porshnev's work on popular uprisings in France was published in French (he had earlier published this work in the Soviet Union in 1948 and in East Germany in 1954). He argued that popular uprisings should be seen as the agency rather than the product of social change, and that in the case of seventeenth-century France they were agencies of reactionary, rather than progressive change. The tax

Figure 26
Robert, Earl of Essex, *from*
Josiah Ricraft, A Survey of
Englands Champions and
Truths faithfull Patriots,
1647.

demands of the monarchy which had provoked the revolts encouraged the bourgeoisie (the middle ranks) not to resist the crown, but to throw in their lot with the nobility to obtain royal offices and to seek tax exemptions by the acquisition of noble status. Porshnev's work was much criticized by Roland Mousnier on the grounds that the purchase of office actually brought the bourgeoisie power and restricted the arbitrary actions of the monarchy. There was no alliance of the nobility and bourgeoisie against the common people, rather, there were social groups 'united by mutual ties of protection and service' (Mousnier, 1977b, p.159). These groups, made up of people of different social orders, were in conflict with the state. He also challenged Porshnev's assumption that seventeenth-century France was a feudal regime, arguing instead that France was a seigneurial regime where seigneurs retained minor powers, the majority of their powers over tenants having been surrendered to the state.

The contribution of classical Marxist history is particularly difficult to assess at present (autumn 1993) when many of its practitioners in the eastern bloc have ceased to publish. Nevertheless, the notion of changing relationships between the social orders informs much more historical explanation than Marxist history alone. Mousnier and his successors use similar categories to Porshnev. It is the relationships between the different social orders which concerns them. Mousnier developed elsewhere the concept of seventeenth-century society as a 'society of orders' where relationships were built on social esteem. This in its turn has been criticized for underplaying the antagonisms present in French society. The privileged orders had more in common with each other and with the crown than they had with the peasantry on whose economic activity they were dependent, argue some of his critics.

Discussions about social status in England have dwelt much more upon social mobility than on class antagonisms. It became clear long ago that there was no simple division on class lines between the supporters of the king and the supporters of parliament. The extent to which it was possible to rise or fall socially has been debated exhaustively but without resolution. It has been argued that in the century before 1640 the gentry rose (R.H. Tawney; Lawrence Stone); the gentry fell (H.R. Trevor-Roper); the aristocracy declined (Lawrence Stone); and the yeomanry rose (W.G. Hoskins). One of the few English historians to have adopted a straightforward class analysis of the English civil war is Brian Manning who has written that the civil war:

> ... was a conflict between rich and poor, strong and weak, ruler and ruled, those who eat their bread in the sweat of other men's brows and those who laboured for their living with their own hands and sold the fruits of their labour. This was the only form which class conflict could take in this type of society at this period of time. (Manning, 1978, p.307)

Increasingly, however, historians' interests have concentrated on local allegiances and patterns of patronage.

In Scotland and Ireland rather different kinds of divisions have been the focus of attention since, to a substantial extent, the final impetus to war was administered from outside the country rather than within. However, Charles I's attempts to reduce the role of the higher nobility in government in Scotland were partly successful.

Economic status

As we saw in Unit 1, economic and social status cannot readily be separated. The acquisition of status depended on a grant of nobility from the crown, but the maintenance of status depended upon a sufficient income to keep up the level of display appropriate to that status. Though sumptuary laws (laws dictating what types of dress and ornament might be worn by people of different social standing) were not enforced in England, there was just as strong a sense there as elsewhere that nobles should dress in a certain way, live in a certain splendour, and employ a certain number of servants.

Historians have been interested in the extent to which the price rises of the later sixteenth century placed the nobility in an adverse position. Lawrence Stone's argument about the decline of the aristocracy was based on an assessment of the incomes of peers. He showed that the average amount of land owned by each peer declined in the late sixteenth century and that, as a result, noble incomes from land fell. To survive economically peers needed either to exploit their possessions in new ways, developing mining for example, or to obtain a pension or trading monopoly from the king.

French nobles were also in difficult economic straits. Apart from the effects of price rises, nobles were affected by the costs of war. Attempts to increase royal revenue from the *taille* by changing the basis of the levy, from the individual to his property, meant that more nobles became liable. Indirect taxes affected them, and the tremendous increase in royal taxes on their tenants meant that tenants found it harder to pay their rents and seigneurial dues. Nobles who stayed at home and exploited their estates by farming their demesne lands directly might make a substantial income. This was the only form of trade in which they might engage without endangering their noble status, but opportunities to do this kind of farming were highly localized to areas where such cash crops as wheat, flax, sheep, and wine might be produced. A position at court or a provincial governorship might well cost its occupant more than it paid him, because of the splendour of the household and entourage he was expected to keep. So, the high nobility in both France and England seems to have experienced some financial difficulties but not insuperable ones, certainly not enough to prompt them to rebellion against the crown.

The Scottish nobility saw Charles I's scheme of 1625 to revoke the title to lands secularized by the church since 1560 and granted to noblemen as a direct attack on them as landowners. Although the scheme failed, it put the Scottish nobility on notice that their privileges were under attack. The early seventeenth century was, for the native Irish nobility, a period of growing indebtedness and economic retreat. Confiscation of their land was compounded by their need to raise funds by selling or mortgaging land to Protestant planters and to the Old English.

Lesser nobility and gentry seem to have fared much as their superiors. Those who could farm their own lands, develop resources or trade did well; those who could not suffered financially. It was amongst merchants that we see some of the most marked differences between the various countries under consideration. Under Richelieu limited efforts were made to promote various economic projects but they came to little, partly because of the neglect of trade under Anne of Austria's regency. The restrictions imposed by France's war effort did little to promote mercantile fortunes. Trading was inimical to the nobility, merchants with social aspirations bought lands for themselves and offices for their sons. The Catholic church disapproved of money-lending and saw the acquisition of wealth as a reprehensible activity.

English merchants bought themselves lands, too, but their prosperity was such that the nobility and gentry sought to share it. Investment in shipping, in the new trading companies such as the East India Company, and in colonial ventures such as the Providence Island Company and the Londonderry Plantation, provided lucrative opportunities for investment. But the merchant élites who ran such operations were not an open group. They were highly oligarchic, based in London and the larger cities, Bristol, Norwich and York, and marrying into each other's families or into the neighbouring gentry. Merchant princes like Baptist Hicks at Chipping Campden (see TV5) were able to enter the landed élite. Many merchants supported parliament during the war, but it is not at all clear that it was economic reasons which prompted them to do so.

Contrast the position of English merchants with that of Scots merchants in the same period. The prosperity immediately following the union of the crowns in 1603 was eroded by a series of poor harvests. A decline in Franco-Scottish trade and trade with northern Germany and the Baltic (largely owing to the Thirty Years' War) reduced merchants' incomes and the returns from customs dues and much crown income went to servicing its debt. Taxation was increased for everyone, but Edinburgh merchants had to make further payments for a new Parliament house and towards the rebuilding of St Giles Cathedral. Furthermore, Scottish trade was increasingly subordinated to English interests as, for example, in the 2 per cent tariff increase which made coal and salt exports from Scotland less competitive. In Ireland, English and, to a lesser extent Scottish, settlers believed themselves to be in a land of opportunity. There was something of a trade boom in the early seventeenth century. Market towns were established or re-established and the trade with England in cattle and sheep was substantial. English and Old English townsmen like the Coppinger family (Video 4) prospered in this period.

We have already, in Unit 1, seen something of the fate of the ordinary taxpayer in this period. The rural and urban poor in France, stretched beyond endurance to pay ever increasing taxes, revolted, though the strength of their objections varied greatly from place to place. In England those dependent on cloth-working suffered with the decline of the market for English woollen cloth. These people lived in the West Country, in East Anglia, the Cotswolds and the West Riding of Yorkshire; but there were already signs that new industries would replace them, notably new types of cloth and the manufacturing of such goods as stockings. We know very little about the economic well being of the common people of Scotland and Ireland.

Economic infrastructure

You can see how economic status may be influenced by factors derived from the general state of the economic infrastructure. In an age before statistics were collected systematically, understanding the structures underlying economic behaviour must largely be a matter of inference from diverse and incomplete sources. In more populous parts of France and the British Isles most wealth was held in the form of land, though in large cities (most of which were also ports) one might find banking, credit and investment. In regions such as the west of Ireland and the western Highlands of Scotland, however, wealth was held in the form of cattle rather than land. Historians using arguments about the underlying structure of the economy, then, have largely to concentrate upon long-term developments.

Arguments about economic change, particularly whether there was an increasing accumulation of capital and institutions to service it, have played more part in assessing the seventeenth century as a whole than in assessing the causes and consequences of the upheavals of the mid-century. The debate centring around work by Robert Brenner is concerned with the extent to which the high rate of peasant proprietorship and sub-division of land-holdings in France meant that there was little incentive for rural proprietors to develop their agriculture beyond the requirements for subsistence or to expand into other enterprises, such as manufacture, which might allow them to accumulate wealth. By contrast, the English rural population, to overcome the increasing homogenization of property rights and accumulation of land by larger proprietors (yeomen), had to find ways of making the land more productive and increasing their incomes, thus developing a form of agrarian capitalism. Brenner's arguments have been challenged, but there has been and continues to be much discussion of the extent to which England was developing 'precocious' capitalist forms. Under this scheme, Scotland, Wales, Ireland and the Pennines are simply seen as economically underdeveloped regions. A book of articles on the debate has no index entry for Wales or Ireland and only a small footnote reference to Scotland (Aston and Philpin, 1985).

Directly and indirectly seventeenth-century states were responsible for a good deal of economic management – through taxes and through the regulation of trade. We have seen how taxes were levied on the sale of many goods and on their transport. Ostensibly, these were devices to raise money for the royal exchequer, but they might also have the effect of encouraging or discouraging the sale, manufacture or import of particular commodities. It was the aim of all seventeenth-century rulers to develop their countries' economies to the point where the countries were economically self-sufficient and able to export surpluses. To this end, we see efforts to create new industries for manufacturing goods which were formerly imported. James VI and I was interested in setting up silk farms, Charles I established the Mortlake tapestry works. Under Richelieu clock-making, gold- and silver-smithing, and gunpowder manufacture were brought under royal control.

The role of the state in these matters can be seen in the petitions presented in England by merchants and manufacturers. For example, in 1641 London merchants complained to parliament of the need to encourage trade and navigation. And in February 1642 'divers gentle-women, citizens' wives, tradesmen's wives and other inhabitants' of London petitioned Queen Henrietta Maria not to leave London.

Another way in which trades were regulated was through corporations, especially urban corporations which had responsibilities for trading standards and employment practices, and had a close relationship with the craft guilds whose members made up the skilled urban workforce. These people might be serious critics of government policy. We have seen how Parisian craftsmen took part in the revolutionary days of August 1648. On the day that Strafford's bill of attainder was sent to the House of Lords with a London petition that justice be executed, several thousand people gathered at Westminster, estimates varied between five and fifteen thousand, shouting 'Justice and execution'. Several commentators referred to the demonstrators as citizens and apprentices including 'citizens of very good account, some worth £30,000, some £40,000' (Manning, 1978, p.25).

We have already seen something of the crown's need for money and the resulting fiscal devices which led in France to popular revolts, and in England to challenges in the courts to the king's attempts to raise money by unparliamentary taxation. The question of royal finances has featured very largely in debates about the breakdown of relations between rulers and ruled in the early seventeenth century. It is perhaps the most obvious common factor between France and England, though the actual reasons for the insufficiency of royal income were different, as were the responses of the taxpayers of the two countries.

It was the haphazard and contingent nature of the royal finances which aroused most opposition. Both monarchs' needs for funds pushed them into a position where they tried to raise money by any means possible. In England and Scotland the expedients provoked opposition, while in France the high level and inequality of the burden were the main issues. Strafford, Laud, Richelieu and Mazarin were unable to set about reforming the tax systems, not least because of the urgency of their need for funds.

Although the French problem was exacerbated by war, it is likely that even without war the French monarchy would have been in similar financial difficulties to the British monarchy, that is to say that ordinary income had ceased to meet the normal expenses of peacetime government. This development transformed relations between governors and governed in the seventeenth century. One of the most important restrictions on both kings' actions was the requirement that taxation be approved in England by parliament, in France by *parlements* and, at regional level, by estates. Immediately that there was a need for permanent rather than occasional taxation, these bodies potentially acquired the right to intervene in the normal conduct of government. As we shall see, however, it did not happen quite like that.

A particularly instructive comparison may be made between the fiscal policies of Charles I and of the revolutionary regimes in England and Scotland. In both countries the tax system was reformed, the level of taxation was raised and distributed much more widely. The governments of the Commonwealth and Protectorate were able to raise very much larger sums by taxation than the monarch had been able to collect.

Politics

Straightforward political history is a less popular research subject now than it has been over the last fifty years or so. However, political explanations remain extremely important and inform much of the work which is being done currently.

The personal finances of chief ministers have been a fruitful area of research, not least because of a general interest in corruption. Studies of the personal finances of Mazarin (Dulong) and Sully (Aristide), and of Wentworth (Kearney) have shown something of the relationship between political power and personal advancement. But more important has been the opening up of the whole question of patronage. It is clear that political advancement operated by means of exchanged favours and personal connections involving family and friends. Peck's work on the early Stuart court and Kettering's work on patrons, brokers and clients in early seventeenth-century France have done much to illuminate the ways in which this system of favour and patronage operated. As Kettering has written:

> The King and his ministers used royal patronage to reward the loyal service of great nobles and their clients, to recruit noble supporters, to appease opponents, and to play off rivals for power, thereby strengthening the royal government and extending its control over France. (Kettering, 1986, p.236)

Kettering has also shown, in an article which might provide a helpful model for historians' work elsewhere, how women were able to exercise patronage. She has shown how French noblewomen, despite their lack of institutional power, extended domestic patronage:

> ... into political, clerical and cultural patronage [which] was sometimes accompanied by considerable economic power. Noblewomen acted as brokers of royal patronage at court and played an important role as brokers of aristocratic patronage. They helped to determine who advanced in their society. (Kettering, 1989, p.841)

This work has extended into a study of noble culture and codes of honour in order to try to understand the psychology of noble revolt in France.

I mention these subjects to show how the definition of 'political' has changed. It is no longer simply used of institutions and formal groupings, but is extended to include the actions of those who, though officially excluded from the 'political nation', are part of the political culture. This notion has informed much of the recent history of popular movements.

Perhaps the most important area of political history to be researched recently has been that of unofficial relationships and groupings and of political relationships in a more regional or local context. The kinds of unofficial grouping which have been studied are the formation of opposition to the crown in the House of Commons, and relations between *noblesse de robe* and *noblesse d'épée*.

Political relationships in the regional and local context have been the subject of attention for a number of reasons. First, there are rich and relatively untapped provincial archives. Second, it is becoming increasingly clear that the relationship between the centre and the localities has much to teach us. The local population made demands of the central government as well as being subject to it and they might do so with or without the intervention of the local administration. People were active

Figure 27
Alexander Lesley, *from Josiah Ricraft,* A Survey of Englands Champions and Truths faithfull Patriots, *1647.*

subjects of both central and local government. Peasant communes in France objected to national officials and taxmen, but might show no animosity to the local nobility. The local nobility might do little to put down peasant revolt, yet try to appease the provincial governor and the royal government. Local administrators in England might be national governors as well by being JPs and MPs. There was then, a three-way relationship which we will explore later in the unit.

Religion

We have already seen in Units 2 and 3 something of the role of religion in the conflicts of the mid-seventeenth century. Bonney (Offprint, 4, p.31) indicates that its role differed markedly from country to country. Rarely were political divisions identical with confessional divisions.

French foreign policy was dictated by the need to contain Habsburg power regardless of whether this meant making alliances with such Protestant powers as the United Provinces (the Netherlands), England or Sweden. James VI and I was far from following a Protestant foreign policy, and Charles I was even further. In domestic politics confessional divisions might be superseded by other claims to loyalty. Many French office-holders were Protestants, but it was the attacks or perceived threats to their position as a privileged caste which provoked their resistance to the crown rather than their position as members of a particular religious group. Rioters who took to the streets in the Protestant cities of La Rochelle and Montauban were defending their privileges rather than their faith. In some places Protestants saw their privileges being jeopardized by rebels. In the prosperous towns of the Garonne valley, Protestants were burgesses and sometimes tax agents and remained loyal to the crown in the insurrections of 1635, 1637, 1643 and during the Frondes.

Even in England, where confessional divisions coincided closely with political divisions in the taking of sides in 1640–2, there was not a complete match. There were possibly only three 'godly' peers, peers with strong Puritan leanings. Russell (1990, p.20) suggests that 'The Parliamentarians in the Lords were largely a court-based group, many of whom seem to have decided that politics was too important to be left to kings'. 'In the Commons', he writes, 'it was a different story: there, the Parliamentarians, with a few exceptions, were those in favour of further reformation.' He estimates that 85 per cent of the members of the House of Commons were committed to further reformation of the church in a more Protestant direction, which means that some 15 per cent of members supported or were prepared to tolerate the Laudian religious reforms.

In England confessional divisions concerned differences over theology, the organization of the church and the extent of lay control. In Scotland, Charles I's attempts to impose the Prayer Book roused furious opposition on the grounds that it was papist and unconstitutional. So the issues there concerned both theology and lay control of the church. However, the ensuing reforms, the National Covenant, the flight of the bishops, and the capturing of shire and burgh government by the Covenanters fused theology and nationalism. The issues in the 1641 rising in Ireland were less clearly theological, though the divisions were confessional. For the English, Roman Catholicism was synonymous with loyalty to the pope above the crown. At moments of pressure this provided the excuse to seize Catholic lands and redistribute them among Protestant settlers. The practice of Catholicism, though technically proscribed, was widespread, though usually fairly private. However, though the English in England regarded Catholics as *ipso facto* traitors, it is far from clear that the English in Ireland did until October 1641. When the rising broke out and Protestant planters were expelled from lands in Ulster which had been appropriated from Catholics earlier in the century, the first act of the Catholic Old English was to offer their help to the government to suppress the rising. Only when this was rejected by the government did they make common cause with the native Irish. Even members of the Catholic Confederation of Kilkenny, the alliance between Old Irish and Old English formed in June 1642, did not regard themselves as rebels: their motto was 'For God, for king, for country'.

During the sixteenth century there were wars in many parts of Europe resulting from the upheavals of which the Protestant and Catholic Reformations formed a part. As with all ostensibly religious wars, other factors played an important role: the strength of monarchies, noble factions and international alliances. Recently, several historians, notably John Morrill for England and Joseph Bergin for France, have argued that the upheavals of mid-seventeenth-century Europe were no more than a continuation of the wars of religion of the sixteenth century. They have rejected the idea that there were new revolutionary forces in favour of the idea that these upheavals were the final stages of an older struggle.

The types of explanation at which we have looked have different parts to play in analysing the mid-seventeenth-century upheavals and the development of the state. Few historians would subscribe to one alone; much of their discussion concerns differences of opinion (backed by their research) about the relative importance of several factors. Before we go on to look at some particular explanations, I'd like to consider a term which, though it cannot properly be said to be a type of explanation, is used to describe the work which some historians are doing on the seventeenth century.

Revisionism

At its most neutral, the term revisionist is simply used to describe those historians who have overturned an accepted orthodoxy, whether it be a school of historians or a set of historical explanations. In this sense it appears simply to mean intellectual iconoclasts, people who deliberately seek to overturn accepted ideas and I suppose that there is something in this. One might, for example, see in this vein the work of Clark (1986, p.130), who argued that 1642 and 1688 did not mark revolutions so much as 'petulant outbursts' in British history.

However, in relation to certain historical debates 'revisionism' has a much more specific meaning. In the context of Irish history the term revisionist refers to those historians who have explored the ambiguities of the Anglo-Irish relationship by using archival sources. The other end of the spectrum (since in these matters we are nearly always dealing with a range of views rather than opposing camps) are those historians who see England's oppression of Ireland as the most powerful force in Ireland's recent history and the purpose of history to chart this relationship and celebrate Ireland's liberation from it.

Figure 28
Edward Massey, *from Josiah Ricraft,* A Survey of Englands Champions and Truths faithfull Patriots, *1647.*

There are revisionists in the history of the English civil war. Crudely, the spectrum ranges between those who see the civil war as having become inevitable only as a result of the politics of Charles I's reign, in particular the breakdown of relations between governors and governed in the 1630s (the revisionists) and those who see the origins of the civil war as lying in long-term structural changes in the economy and social organization of the country, some of which had begun as much as a century earlier. I emphasize that this is a spectrum of opinion because there are several revisionists who recognize that religion was a fundamentally divisive subject, especially if the broader view of the civil wars of the British Isles is taken. Conrad Russell is often identified as a leading revisionist for his work on the early Stuart parliaments, John Morrill for his work on local communities, and Kevin Sharpe for his work on Charles I's personal rule. But, and here is the reason why I emphasize the idea of a spectrum of opinion, few revisionists would deny that religious divisions (though their cause is widely debated) were much more long-standing than Charles I's financial problems.

There has not been quite the same wholesale attempt to rewrite the history of the causes of the Frondes as there has been for the history of the causes of the English civil war. However, where we do find revisionists is in the consideration of Louis XIV's absolutism – we shall consider this in Units 12 and 16. There is now a school of historians who would argue that absolutism in the sense of untrammelled royal power was never achieved, that Louis XIV's freedom of action was always restricted and that he regarded himself as under the law rather than above it.

Having looked at the types of explanation which historians of the seventeenth century use, let us consider how Briggs and Coward use them. The first section of each book is concerned with setting up the social, economic, political and religious background to the civil wars, by now you have read most of this.

Exercise Read Briggs, pp.122–9 and Coward, pp.185–204, for a discussion of the immediate causes for the breakdown of relations between governors and governed. What kinds of explanation do Briggs and Coward favour?

Discussion Both historians refer to a great many kinds of explanation because these are textbooks and are necessarily concerned to represent a variety of opinion. The consideration of single issues appears more in historical monographs and articles in specialist historical journals. Briggs and Coward have both contributed to this kind of specialist literature so we might expect their general discussion to favour some kinds of explanation rather than others.

There are a number of places where each author indicates where his chief concerns lie. Let us start with Briggs. It is tempting to think that he is not much concerned with religion except as a source of political division, but in fact he deals with this in his final chapter. In addition, in the introduction he announces himself as a social historian and in chapters 1 and 2 he concentrates upon social and economic conditions. Much of his discussion of economic conditions is in the context of their impact upon the balance of social and economic privilege. There is some discussion of the economic infrastructure, but chiefly in relation to price rises and wages and their effect on social conditions. In his discussion of shorter-term problems, Briggs is much concerned with the balance of

demands on the monarchy between noble cliques, foreign war and raising the funds to pacify the one and sustain the other. So, of our types of
explanation I would say that Briggs was concerned chiefly with social and
economic status, to a lesser degree with economic infrastructure, and sees
religion as playing relatively little part in the breakdown of relations
between governors and governed. He has some concern with politics,
with the political impact of peasant revolts, the defence of noble privilege
and the need to reorganize royal administration to improve its financial
position. However, he gives us virtually no history of political relationships within the government and amongst the rulers, nor does he discuss
institutions. I think it is fair to say, too, that he is not expounding a general thesis about the nature of early modern French society. (Elsewhere
in his book he indicates his own dissent from arguments put forward by
other historians as, for example, on pp.80, 82, 90, 99–100, 103 and 105–6.)

Coward, like Briggs, sets out his stall in the introduction, he then
elaborates on his ideas in the introduction to the main sections. He is chiefly concerned with political, constitutional, religious and ecclesiastical divisions in English society, though he wishes to set them in their social, economic and intellectual context. He has a rather more obvious argument to
develop than has Briggs. He is concerned with the constitution as a working structure, as a substantially harmonious whole, though one which is
subject to constant movement. He believes that 'the political inadequacies
of the king and the pressure of events after 1640' go a long way to providing an explanation but that events were also influenced by attitudes
formed in the decades before 1640, notably godly reformation (pp.186–7).

In general, Briggs shows a concern for long-term causes, 'an understanding of the earlier period is vital for any explanation of the *ancien régime* as
a whole' (p.2). He rejects Porshnev's class analysis of the divisions in
French society, but comments in another book that the French government appealed to urban and rural notables to defend the established
order in the 1630s and 1640s which they generally did, even if they had
earlier made common cause with popular forces in opposing new tax
demands (Briggs, 1989, p.168). Coward is influenced by Conrad Russell
in his emphasis on the short term and political. Russell has recently
restated his view that:

> ... it has become painfully clear that it is impossible to interpret the
> Civil War as the clash of two clearly differentiated social groups or
> classes: the fullest possible knowledge of men's social and economic
> background, if it leaves out the preaching available in their home
> parishes, tells us nothing about their likely allegiance in the Civil
> War. (Russell, 1990, p.2)

Both Briggs and Coward, despite their differences of approach, have a
common view of the significance of external wars in prompting the
deterioration of relations between governors and governed and in dividing the governors. Briggs shows how the politics of tax demands finally
alienated the *parlementaires* and Coward how the need to call parliament,
first to find money for wars with the Scots and then for money to quell
the Irish rising, precipitated the deterioration of relations.

Particular and local explanations of the civil wars

In this section I want to concentrate on explanations of the civil wars specific to the individual countries. Explanations were forthcoming from the first days after the wars were ended (I distinguish between historians looking back and commentators analysing the causes at the time). Louis XIV was quite clear that the principal cause of the Frondes was too close a relationship between the great nobles and the judges of the *parlement*. Charles I was not able to pass a retrospective judgement and Charles II was too canny to do so.

But other commentators expressed their views freely.

Exercise   Read *Anthology*, I.19 and 20. To what does each of these writers attribute the civil wars in his own country?

Discussion   Bossuet, an ardent royalist, seems to suggest that it was noble factions who were responsible for the troubles in France. For Clarendon it was preachers who inflamed the people to rebellion, not the parliament. It was ministers who spoke against both church and state and justified rebellion.

Bossuet was very well connected with the French nobility and he was reluctant to place the blame upon Condé's perversity. He makes no reference to popular discontents. Clarendon, as well connected but writing after he had fallen from royal favour, is rather more considered and, in his great multi-volume work offers various other contributory factors to the outbreak of the war, the personality of the king, for example. Charles, Clarendon wrote:

> ... had an excellent understanding, but was not confident enough of it; which made him often times change his own opinion for a worse, and follow the advice of a man that did not judge so well as himself. And this made him more irresolute than the conjuncture of his affairs would admit. If he had been of a rougher and more imperious nature, he would have found more respect and duty. (Clarendon, 1888, vol. IV, p.490)

Bossuet, in his sermon at the funeral of Henrietta Maria in 1669, passed comment on the role of religion in the English civil war, which he saw as a dreadful kind of anarchy, 'no limits to licence; laws abolished; ... usurpation and tyranny going under the name of freedom', as well as the multitude of sects (Bossuet, 1888, pp.112, 126).

Increasingly, in both France and England the search for explanations for the civil wars is being conducted by means of local studies, looking at the pressures within local communities and at the tensions between them, the larger community and the national government. Scotland and Ireland are being less studied in this way partly because much of the basic national history of the period is not well researched and, in the case of Ireland, there is a serious shortage of materials.

These local studies in England and France are not merely local history, they deliberately set out to establish smaller communities within a national economic, social, political and religious context. They also explore the relationships between local populations, local governors and royal government.

Exercise   Please read Dewald (Offprint 5). How does Dewald characterize the place of the Norman nobility in seventeenth-century French society?

Discussion   We are given here details of only one family (Roncherolles), and we would need information about other families to know how characteristic they were. But we can see here clearly how the complex relationship between the central government, the local government and the local population operated. Roncherolles was a member of the Estates General (the national assembly). The family, as *noblesse d'epée*, also considered themselves to have a particular relationship with the crown, but not necessarily one of quiet obedience. They felt themselves able to object to measures to establish peace taken by royal officials and judges, and that they were in the position of conferring favours on the crown, as well as receiving them. Roncherolles was able to barter his loyalty to Mazarin, an important ingredient of which was the network of relationships of which he was a part: ties of patronage, clientage and cousinage. Dewald, the author, distinguishes between different levels of nobility – there is the Norman nobility of which the Roncherolles family was a part and there were *'les grands'*, the great families, courtiers, close to the king, recipients of such posts as provincial governorships. (Briggs makes a similar distinction on pp.112–4, though he does not do so in his discussion of social status at the beginning of the book.)

Roncherolles' remarks about status show us how clearly French nobles perceived their status and regarded it as something to be defended. But note how he distinguishes between different kinds of nobility. It was not the antiquity of a noble title that was the issue, it was the source of the honour. Plainly ancient ideas about valour play a significant part in the perception of 'true' nobility, and in establishing its relation to the crown.

Dewald does not offer us any reasons for the nobility to take one side or the other in the Frondes, rather he shows how ambiguous the provincial nobility's position was and how the issues were not clear cut, in this instance the Norman nobles supported the crown but, given a slightly different balance of factors they might have come out against it.

Exercise   Turn now to Coward pp.204–7, which you read for Unit 3. How does Dewald's approach compare with Coward's?

Discussion   Dewald is writing a monograph about Norman society while Coward is synthesizing the work of a number of historians, there are footnotes to Holmes's work on East Anglia and Cliffe's work on Yorkshire.

Both historians write about the complexity of social divisions in the local community and of how people took up sides for a wide variety of reasons, some of them extremely local, some of them of more general concern. This complexity of relationships is highlighted in relations with the central government. Coward warns us not to see Westminster politics in isolation (p.206) and Dewald (p.38) refers to the competing claims for the loyalties of the Norman nobility.

Let us now turn to an extract from one of the more important English local studies, on Warwickshire.

Exercise   Please read Offprint 6. How does Hughes's approach differ from Coward's?

Discussion   Hughes's chief point of difference with Coward is in her perception that the divisions which coalesced into those between supporters of the king and supporters of parliament were a long time in the making. She uses for this the evidence of the development of opposition to the ship money levies, both in the county government's increased difficulty in collecting the tax and in the opposition to new methods of levying the tax.

The essential point of difference between Hughes and Coward is that whilst Coward sees the opposition to the king really only forming after the meeting of parliament in 1640, Hughes sees it as developing slowly over a longer period and in a not very clearly expressed way in the localities.

In Offprints 5 and 6 we have seen how historians of the written word have used documents to analyse the breakdown of relations between governors and governed. But there are other ways of measuring how people perceived stability. Buildings can give us an extremely important idea about whether people felt themselves to be secure or threatened.

Material evidence for perceptions of stability

In this section I want to develop the suggestions made in TV4 about the extent to which people felt a need to build defensively, looking in particular at early seventeenth-century Ireland. Now start work on video 4, this should take you about thirty minutes.

I shall start by giving you some information about the builders and the location of the three buildings we are going to study. Then you should view the first section of the tape, you will be told when to stop. You should then work on the exercise and return to the second part of the tape for the discussion.

Dalway's Bawn, near Carrickfergus, co. Antrim, Northern Ireland

J. Dalway or Dalloway was an Englishman who went to Ireland as an officer in the Earl of Essex's army in the late sixteenth century. Mayor of Carrickfergus in 1592 and 1600, he received considerable grants of land in east Antrim and it was said that he occupied ten square miles between Carrickfergus and Ballynure. In 1608 he received a further grant; the government stipulating that he had to build there a house or castle of stone or brick with a bawn (walled enclosure). He seems only to have built a timber house, but it was reported in 1632 that he had spent £32 for each of four flankers (towers).

The bawn is separated from any settlement. Ulster did not have English-style villages and the norm for the plantation was dispersed settlements. There were some differences between English and Scots settlements, the Scots' more closely resembling those of the native Irish with dispersed fields and clusters of farms (clachans) whilst the English tended to have consolidated land holdings.

Figure 29
Mullagh, detail from a map by Thomas Raven. Reproduced by permission of the North Down Heritage Centre, Bangor.

Figure 30
*Map of Ireland showing
location of houses shown in
the video.*

Monea Castle, co. Fermanagh, Northern Ireland

The Revd Malcolm Hamilton, a Scottish planter, Rector of Devenish and
Archbishop of Cashel 1623–9 (in the Church of Ireland), built the castle
in 1618. He was deeply opposed to any idea of tolerating Catholicism. In
1688 the castle was the residence of Gustavus Hamilton (no relation),
governor of Enniskillen which was an important garrison town nearby.

West Ulster was a wild area in which there had been little penetration by English or Scots planters and where the O'Neills were still
very powerful rulers. Not until after the 1650s did this part of Ulster
become much settled by English and Scots.

Coppinger's Court, near Ross Carbery, co Cork, Republic of Ireland

Coppinger's Court was built in 1618 by Alderman John Coppinger, a
member of an Old English family from Cork city, whose interests
extended outside the city in the early seventeenth century. John Coppinger and his nephew Walter bought lands in west Cork from penurious
Gaelic Irish families. Apart from building this house, Coppinger granted
10 leases of lands round Baltimore to new English settlers with a view to
establishing a market town. At his death in 1639 the town of Baltimore
continued a precarious existence as a new English settlement with his son
Dominic as the Old English landlord. .

West Cork was a predominantly Old English region, but during the
seventeenth century, with the Munster settlement in which the Boyle family (Earls of Cork) were so important, land increasingly passed to newer
English settlers.

Having read the accounts of the builders of these houses and noted
their location now look at Video 4, Part 1 to learn about the buildings
themselves.

Video Exercise

With this information write notes on how each building reflects the
cumstances in which it was built.

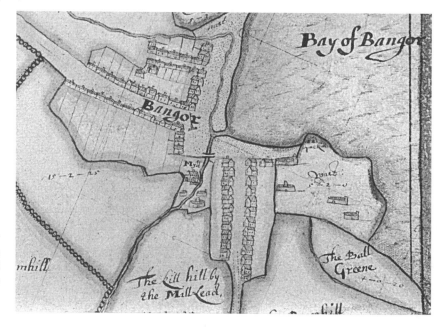

Figure 31
Bangor, *detail from a map by
Thomas Raven. Reproduced
by permission of the North
Down Heritage Centre,
Bangor.*

Discussion   Watch Part 2 of the video for the discussion.

General explanations

Increasingly in studying the mid-seventeenth-century conflicts historians are trying to use the evidence of what was happening in local communities to build up a picture of what was happening across the whole country, taking into account regional variation and local loyalties. But these studies do not prevent there being attempts at grand theories.

A number of historians have tried to account for the fact that in the mid-seventeenth century many European countries experienced major political, social, economic and religious upheavals. They have offered a variety of global explanations such as the weather, epidemic disease, the transition from feudalism to capitalism as causes but none has found much support. In this section I shall look briefly at the 'general crisis' thesis and at the concept of multiple kingdoms, as attempts to provide general explanations.

The 'general crisis' thesis

Whilst everyone can agree that war was widespread in mid-seventeenth-century Europe, they have not been able to agree upon why there was a crisis which led to war. The crisis of mid-seventeenth-century Europe has been redescribed as an extension of the crisis of the 1590s and as part of a world-wide crisis (including the time of troubles in Russia, the overthrow of the Ming dynasty by Manchus in China, and the establishment of the Tokugawa shogunate in Japan). It has been seen as having numerous consequences, such as changes in gender relations and the structure of the family. And several features have been seen as both causes and consequences, for example the emergence of a class of people who accumulated capital by trading and who reinvested their wealth in commercial or industrial enterprises, or the call for political rights by those who had acquired wealth but who were excluded from traditional political processes.

Eric Hobsbawm's articulation in 1954 of a general economic crisis has received less detailed attention than Hugh Trevor-Roper's articulation of 1959:

> ... a crisis not of the constitution nor of the system of production, but of the State, or rather, of the relation of the State to society. Different countries found their way out of the crisis in different ways ... in Holland, France and England, the crisis marked the end of an era: the jettison of a top-heavy superstructure, the return to responsible, mercantilist policy. For by the seventeenth century the Renaissance courts had grown so great, had consumed so much in 'waste',

and had sent their multiplying suckers so deep into the body of society, that they could only flourish for a limited time, and in a time, too, of expanding general prosperity. When that prosperity failed, the monstrous parasite was bound to falter. (Aston, 1974, pp.94–5)

Trevor-Roper's article generated considerable debate in the journal *Past and Present* and elsewhere. It provoked responses from historians of a number of countries including France, though it does not seem to have had much impact upon debates within France.

Roland Mousnier, historian of French institutions, characterized Trevor-Roper's crisis as a rising of the country against the court and the bureaucratic apparatus and argued that in France it was office-holders, members of the bureaucratic apparatus, who helped to provoke revolt. He rejects the idea of a crisis in relations between state and society as being founded on 'inadequate analysis' (Aston, 1974, p.104).

Another thesis suggests that as the early modern state was, in large part, a military institution, often spending as much as half of its income on war, the economic crisis was the result of military spending. The increase in the cost of keeping an army far outstripped the increase in revenue and led to a crisis in royal finances and security. Figures for France and England certainly suggest that there was a great increase in military manpower.

	France	England
1550s	50,000 men	20,000 men
1590s	80,000 men	30,000 men
1630s	150,000 men	–
1650s	100,000 men	70,000 men

Source: Parker and Smith, 1985, p.14; © 1978 G. Parker and L. M. Smith.

Price inflation meant that the cost of each soldier rose four-fold between 1530 and 1630 with the result that no government could afford to go to war but that all governments were forced into it.

The general crisis thesis has not produced any single satisfactory explanation, but it has had the effect of stimulating historians to think about setting the history of individual countries in a broader context. An interesting illustration of this is the contribution made to the debate by Maurice Lee writing about Scotland. He suggests that:

One of the advantages of doing research on a less than major state such as Scotland is that the temptation to magnify findings is minimised ... [but] what happened, and did not happen, in Scotland is a matter of great importance for the validity of any theory of general crisis. (Lee, 1984, pp.137–8)

Lee argues that the crisis in Scotland in 1637 was purely the result of the king's religious policies there. This in turn led to the calling of the Long Parliament and thus to the outbreak of the civil war in England. Without the king's provocation of the Scots there might not have been wars in England and Scotland. Without these British examples, he argues, the general crisis thesis is untenable because most of the other European conflicts can be attributed to the Thirty Years' War.

I would counter Lee's argument by saying that the problems in Ireland were just as much to blame and would have necessitated calling a parliament in England, had one not already been called because of the Scottish problems. However, Lee's argument does demonstrate that England cannot be seen in isolation in this period, the civil wars may justly be called the war of the three kingdoms. And recently such English historians as Conrad Russell, Ronald Hutton and John Morrill have considered what they refer to as the 'British context' of the English civil war. Russell has gone furthest in his analysis and has gone some way to offering a more general thesis, that of multiple kingdoms.

Multiple kingdoms

In Unit 1 we looked at the structures of the state in France and the British Isles and saw how we might describe the British Isles as a multiple kingdom and France as a composite kingdom.

It is Conrad Russell who has done most to publicize the idea of the multiple kingdom as being one of the causes of structural weakness in England which ultimately gave rise to the civil war. Scotland was certainly constitutionally on a par with England, so you might say that it was the very failure to understand that Scotland was part of a multiple kingdom and not an English colony which led to the basic policy mistakes which sparked off the Bishops' Wars. Likewise, if Ireland had not been subject to policies devised in Whitehall and implemented through the English administration in Dublin which led to a coalition of the Catholic Irish with the hitherto loyal but Catholic Old English, the conflagration there might not have come about or might at least have been contained.

Exercise   Read Offprint 7. How does Russell characterize the problem of multiple kingdoms as a cause of the English civil war?

Discussion   Russell particularly identifies Charles I's misplaced attempts to harmonize the three kingdoms of England, Scotland and Ireland and his lack of understanding of Scotland and Ireland. But it was essentially the *combination* of the revolts that he provoked in those countries with religious problems and the financial pressures of the military revolution which finally led to war.

Two questions arise from this Russell extract. First, have we not encountered Russell as the arch-exponent of the short-term and accidental origins of the English civil war? And, second, how does this notion of multiple kingdoms have a more general application?

In answer to the first question, Russell emphasizes the importance of Charles I's personality, certainly a short-term and particular cause and he is certain that in 1637, before the Prayer Book revolt in Scotland, civil war was 'not visibly imminent', but that of all the things Charles might have done to provoke a revolution, trying to force the Anglican Prayer Book on Scotland was the likeliest catalyst.

In answer to the second I can do no better than to quote Professor Russell's inaugural lecture given in London in 1985, the first major public airing of his ideas about multiple kingdoms. We have encountered in Unit 1 the idea of the British Isles as a multiple kingdom and France as a composite kingdom. Here Russell is drawing upon one of the anomolies in France, the king was ruler of Béarn as king of Navarre, so France was in this particular instance both a composite and a multiple monarchy.

When three kingdoms under one ruler all take to armed resistance within three years, it seems sensible to investigate the possibility that their actions may have had some common causes. We will not find them in constitutional development, for their constitutional structures were profoundly different. We will not find them in their social systems, for they were even more different: a social history of Britain in the early seventeenth century would be a stark impossibility. However, there are two obvious types of cause which are common to all three kingdoms. One is that they were all ruled by Charles I. It is perhaps fair to paraphrase Lady Bracknell, and so say that 'to lose one kingdom might happen to any king, but to lose three savours of carelessness'.

The other thing all three kingdoms have in common is that they are all parts of a multiple monarchy of three kingdoms. We now know, thanks to a large body of work, that the relations between multiple kingdoms were among the main causes of instability in continental Europe, and Professors Elliott and Koenigsberger have been asking for some time whether the rule which applies across the Channel also applied in Britain. This article is intended to suggest that the answer to their question is 'yes'.

Thanks to them and many others, we now know a good deal about the normal flashpoints in multiple monarchies. They include resentment at the king's absence and about the disposing of offices, the sharing of costs of war and the choice of foreign policy problems of trade and colonies, and the problems of foreign intervention. All these causes of difficulty were present in Britain. It is particularly interesting that Secretary Coke, probably in 1627–8, drew up a plan for a British version of Olivares' union of arms, and that the Scots in 1641 were demanding the right to trade with English colonies. Yet these issues are surprisingly peripheral: it is possible to find them if we look for them, but only in Anglo-Irish relations between 1625 and 1629 does one of them (in this case the cost of war) become a central theme. The absence of wars for much of the period between 1603 and 1640, and the overwhelming preponderance of the English revenue over those of Scotland and Ireland both contribute to this comparative silence.

This leaves only one of the normal causes of trouble within multiple kingdoms, that caused by religion. This one issue alone accounted for almost all the difficulties between the kingdoms of Britain between 1637 and 1642, and it caused enough trouble to leave very little room for any others. Some of the trouble seems to have arisen from the fact that religion for Charles, like arms for Olivares, was the issue on which he chose to press for greater uniformity. In Britain, as in the Spanish monarchy, it is the issue on which the centre demanded uniformity on which the liberties and privileges of the outlying kingdoms are most loudly asserted.

The rare cases in Europe of multiple kingdoms with different religions do not suggest that the British reaction is disproportionate. One case is that of France and Béarn, where Louis XIII, discovering, to his dismay, that he was King of the Protestant kingdom of Béarn (part of Henri IV's old kingdom of Navarre), decided to invade it and suppress it, even at the risk of war with Spain. The most famous case of multiple kingdoms with different religions is that of Spain and the Netherlands, and that produced disturbances on the same scale as the British. Britain, moreover, offered the peculiar and illogical combination of difference of religions with a theory of authority in the king as supreme head of the church. A British king who presided over different religions thus offered a built-in challenge to his own authority, something which Charles I was never likely to accept with equanimity. Though there are other cases in Europe in which one king presided over two religions, I am aware of none in which a single king presided over three. Moreover, Britain appears to be a unique case of multiple kingdoms all of which were internally divided in religion, and in all of which there existed a powerful group which preferred the religion of one of the others to their own. Perhaps the problem we ought to be trying to solve is not why this situation produced an explosion under Charles, but how James succeeded in presiding over it for 23 years without one. (Russell, 1987, pp.397–8; reproduced from Russell, C. (1987), 'The British problem and the English Civil War', *History, The Journal of the Historical Association*, Vol. 72, No. 236, October 1987, The Historical Association.)

You will notice that Russell's chief example of a multiple kingdom, apart from Britain, is Spain. His reference to France as a multiple monarchy is in respect of Navarre, the most recently acquired territory which was united with France when Henri IV inherited the French throne in 1589. However, differences of jurisdiction between territories ruled by the same rulers were certainly a major cause of instability in the mid-seventeenth century. We might argue that the efforts of successive French kings to diminish the independence of the *pays d'état* or to reduce the privileges of Protestant enclaves caused conflict (though the kings themselves argued that it was to restore order out of existing conflict that they sought to extend royal control over them). I do not myself think that this is a sufficient explanation for the Frondes, however, which concerned the defence of sectional privileges rather regional separatism.

Conclusion

This unit was intended to show you that ascribing causes to complex events is itself a complicated business. Historians are not simply wilful or the victims of fashion in the kinds of cause they dwell on, but there is a constant interaction between existing scholarship, current research and the concerns of the present which leads us to re-examine old questions anew.

References

Aston, T. (1974), *Crisis in Europe 1560–1660: Essays from Past and Present*, Routledge and Kegan Paul, London.

Aston, T. and Philpin, C.H.E. (eds) (1985), *The Brenner Debate: Agrarian Class Structure and Economic Development in Pre-Industrial Europe*, Cambridge University Press, Cambridge.

Bercé, Y.–M. (1990), *History of Peasant Revolts: The Social Origins of Rebellion in Early Modern France*, Polity, Cambridge.

Bergin, J. (1991) 'European history 1598–1715' in *Annual Bulletin of Historical Literature*, 75, Historical Association, pp.61–70.

Bonney, R. (1988), *Society and Government in France under Richelieu and Mazarin 1624–61*, Macmillan, London.

Bossuet, J.–B. (1988), *Oraisons funèbres: Édition Corrigée et augmentée d'un sommaire bibliographique*, Bordas, Paris.

Briggs, R. (1989), *Communities of Belief: Cultural and Social Tensions in Early Modern France*, Clarendon Press, Oxford.

Brown, K.M. (1992), *Kingdom or Province? Scotland and the Regal Union 1603–1715*, Macmillan, London.

Canny, N. (1987), *From Reformation to Restoration: Ireland 1534–1660*, Helicon, Dublin.

Clarendon, E. (1888), *The History of the Rebellion and Civil Wars in England*, edited by W.D. Macray, Clarendon Press, Oxford, 6 vols.

Clark, J.C.D. (1986), *Revolution and Rebellion: State and Society in England in the Seventeenth and Eighteenth Centuries*, Cambridge University Press, Cambridge.

Guizot, F. (1890), *History of the English Revolution of 1640*, translated by William Hazlitt, London.

Ireland (1641), *The Last Newes from Ireland being a Relation of the Hostile and Bloody Proceeding of the Rebellious Papists There*, London.

Kettering, S. (1986), *Patrons, Brokers and Clients in Seventeenth-Century France*, Oxford University Press, New York.

Kettering, S. (1989), 'The patronage power of early modern French noblemen', *Historical Journal*, 32, pp.817–41.

Lee, M. (1984), 'Scotland and the 'General Crisis' of the Seventeenth Century', *Scottish Historical Review*, 63, pp.136–54.

Manning, B. (1978), *The English People and the English Revolution*, Penguin, Harmondsworth. (First published by Heinemann, 1976.)

Morrill, J.S. (1976), *The Revolt of the Provinces: Conservatives and Radicals in the English Civil War 1630–1650*, George Allen and Unwin, London.

Morrill, J.S. (1993), *The Nature of the English Revolution*, Longman, London.

Mousnier, R. (1977a), 'Some reasons for the Fronde', the revolutionary days in Paris in 1648', in P.J. Coveney (ed.), *France in Crisis 1620–1675*, Macmillan, London. (Mousnier's article appeared originally in French in 1949.)

Mousnier, R. (1977b), 'Research into popular uprisings in France before the Fronde', in P.J. Coveney (ed.), *France in Crisis 1620–1675*, Macmillan, London. (This article appeared originally in French in 1958.)

Parker, G. and Smith, L.M. (1985), *The General Crisis of the Seventeenth Century*, Routledge and Kegan Paul, London.

Proceedings (1641), *The heads of Several Proceedings in both Houses of Parliament, from the 29 of November to the 6 of December 1641*, London.

Richardson, R.C. (1977), *The Debate on the English Revolution*, Methuen, London.

Russell, C. (1987), 'The British Problem and the English Civil War', *History*, 72, pp.395–415.

Unit 5
The return to internal stability

Prepared for the course team by
Arthur Marwick

Contents

Study timetable

Weeks of study	Texts	Video	AC	Set books
2	Unit 5; *Anthology*, I.21–27; Offprints 8, 9, 10; Illustration Book	Video 5		Coward, Briggs

During the period of this unit you will also need to watch TV7 and 8.

Objectives

By the end of this unit you should:

1   have firmly in mind a clear outline of the main political, religious, and economic development and trends, from the end of the English civil war (1649) to the end of the first stage of the Restoration settlement (1665) in the British Isles, and from the end of the Frondes (1653) to the establishment of Louis XIV's personal rule and completion of the financial reforms of Colbert (1669) in France;

2   be able to identify the main topics of contention (e.g. taxation, religion, ambitions of powerful local leaders) standing in the way of the restoration of stability in our period of study, and to discuss in an informed way how far, and in what manner, they were resolved;

3   be able to identify the immediate consequences of the Frondes and the civil war, both with regard to princes and governments and to the less privileged, including women;

4   be able to discuss critically the legacies of the Frondes and the civil wars as they manifested themselves in France and the British Isles during our period, and to assess how far they contributed to stability or instability;

5   be able to make informed comparisons and contrasts between developments in the four countries with a view to establishing which were common phenomena and which reflected of particular characteristics of the individual countries.

You will also find material on the results of the Frondes in the offprint, R. Knecht, *The Fronde*.

Outline of developments and trends: British Isles, 1649–60

England

Together we are going to work through chapter 7 of Coward: mostly I will be asking questions, for which I will provide specimen answers, but sometimes I will simply ask you to write down certain points for yourself. You should note right away that while Coward decided to call the previous chapter 'The making of the English revolution', he calls this one 'The failure of revolution'. Historians put a lot of thought into choosing the titles of their chapters and sections of chapters: these are as much indications of areas for discussion as of final conclusions. A lot of thought, too, goes into how a book is structured into chapters, and chapters into sections. After a general introductory paragraph, this chapter breaks into a number of sections and sub-sections, totalling twelve in all. This makes it very easy to secure a firm outline of the successive phases of republican government.

Exercise   1   (a) Coward identifies two sets of aspirations, one tending to further upheaval, one to stability. What are these? (b) How near did the republican regimes come to establishing permanent stability? To achieve this what was required?

2   'The search for "godly reformation".' (a) Be sure that you have got clear in your own mind the names of the different radical groups and what they stood for. (b) What was the reaction of the political nation to their programmes?

3   'Conservatism and the Rump'. (a) What constitutional changes did the Rump enact? (b) What reforms did it carry through? (c) What repressive measures was it responsible for?

4   'Reasons for the Rump's conservatism'. (a) What two crises did the Rump face at the outset? (b) What older myths about the Rump does Coward challenge?

5   'The Rump's achievements'. (a) What was the Rump's most notable achievement? (b) With regard to stability, what is the significance of this achievement?

6   'The dissolution of the Rump'. What was the fundamental reason behind Cromwell's getting rid of the Rump?

7   'Oliver Cromwell'. This is a masterly brief discussion of the problems involved in analysing the character and achievements of Cromwell. Be sure to digest carefully what Coward is saying.

8   'The Barebones Parliament, July–December, 1653'. We now move to the next (brief) phase of the political chronology. (a) Was the Barebones Parliament a true parliament? (b) Why did Cromwell feel that the Barebones Parliament could not be allowed to continue?

9   'Cromwellian government, 1653–8'. Now we are into a major new political phase, divided by Coward into several sub-sections. Here he begins with a one-paragraph overview, mentioning the royalist

revolts of the mid-fifties and of August 1659, but insisting that there was no break-down in government.

10   'The achievements of Cromwellian government'. (a) What is the major constitutional document establishing the Protectorate? (b) What class of people did the regime come to depend on more and more in the localities, and what was Cromwell always careful not to offend? (c) Coward suggests there was a brief interlude in which these processes were interrupted. What was this? (d) What appear to be Cromwell's two greatest achievements – one admired even by Cromwell's enemies, the other singled out by Coward?

11   'The failures of Cromwellian government'. (a) What was the fundamental cause of Cromwell's failure? (b) What was the major threat to stability during this phase? (c) What three hated elements did the rule of the major-generals represent? (d) What constitutional document replaced the Instrument of Government? How did the new form of government differ from the one it replaced?

12   'The end of the Good Old Cause, 1658–60'. Coward's final sentence links back to the opening paragraph of the chapter. The Commonwealth, and the Protectorate under Oliver, he argues, were successful in maintaining stability, but, in the confusion following Oliver's death, stability collapsed, making, Coward says, restoration of the monarchy inevitable. Now two questions for you. (a) Why did Richard Cromwell lose the support of the army? (b) What parts were played by the army and by sections and individuals within the army in the collapse of republican government?

Specimen Answers and   1   (a) The demands of the army and religious sects for further
Discussion   sweeping reforms, and the desire of the pre-civil war rulers in the localities for the restoration of stability. (b) Very near, seems to be Coward's answer. A combination of revolutionary radicalism and conservative traditionalism. You don't, of course, have to accept Coward's views. He obviously has a very deep understanding of, and sympathy for, the republican experiments; and he is very aware of the unpopularity of the Stuarts. Yet it may be that the tension between radicalism and traditionalism was too strong to allow for permanent stability. Perhaps, too, Coward slightly underestimates the very powerful sense of the 'naturalness' of monarchy (though perhaps anything can begin to seem natural in time). Finally, it does seem to me to become very clear towards the end of the chapter that all of the regimes were ultimately dependent on the army – could one have permanent stability on that basis?

2   (a) This one was for you alone. (b) 'Horror' (p.238).

3   (a) House of Lords and monarchy abolished. Council of State established. Engagement instituted. England declared a Commonwealth. (You may, very reasonably have said more, but to me these are the basic features.) (b) Repealed compulsory church attendance. Some reforms in law. (c) Repression of Levellers. Reintroduction of press censorship. Severe measures against radical sects and against adultery, swearing, etc.

4 Severe economic crisis. (Though it is difficult, in the seventeenth century, to speak of 'economic recovery', the immediate crisis did pass quite quickly.) Threat of invasion launched from Ireland. (b) That all the Presbyterians (i.e. moderates) had already been excluded from it; and that all the Independents (religious radicals) were political radicals.

5 (a) It made republican government tolerable enough to be stable. (b) It convinced enough people of its legitimacy to ensure its own continuation.

6 The Rump no longer had the support of the army, and Cromwell felt bound to side with the army.

7 Another one for you alone.

8 (a) No: it was nominated, not elected. (b) Because the activities of the radical minority were alienating moderate opinion.

9 It is for you to absorb this sub-section.

10 (a) The Instrument of Government. (b) The 'established gentry'; 'respectable local opinion'. (c) The interlude of the major-generals. (d) Foreign policy; religious toleration.

11 (a) He was dependent on the army as he wished to achieve his aim of a godly reformation. (b) Penruddock's Rising of March 1655 (This is important, and I'll discuss it later). (c) Centralization, high taxation, and army rule. (d) The (amended) Humble Petition and Advice. It was a parliamentary, anti-military constitution, reverting to a two-chamber parliament. (You may, very properly, have said more; but I think that is the essence.)

12 (a) He relied heavily on civilian Cromwellians. (b) Pressured by radical elements in the junior ranks, the army leaders forced the dissolution of parliament and the recall of the Rump. They then replaced the Rump with a Committee of Safety headed by Fleetwood. But when the army in Scotland under Monck, supported by the armies in Yorkshire (under Fairfax) and Ireland, and the navy in the Downs, Fleetwood resigned in panic. After marching south to London, Monck perceived that neither the Rump nor the army was capable of ruling, and that there was no alternative to opening initiatives towards the return of the Stuarts. (No doubt you will not have expressed it exactly like that. However, if you have not got the sequence of events clear in your mind, go back and read the final sub-section of Coward's chapter again.)

Scotland to 1660

The Scots played an important part in the outbreak of the civil war and the Scottish Presbyterians made common cause with the English parliamentarians. However, differences quickly appeared. Coward does not say much about Scotland, so you should turn to Offprint 8. Read from the beginning through to the end of chapter 3 and on to the end of the first paragraph of chapter 4, then do the exercise below. Note that the pro-royalist Scottish aristocrats are referred to as 'the Whig Ascendancy' in this offprint.

Exercise   1   What four armies were still in contention in Scotland after the English civil war had ended? Which one won?

2   In what sense was stability established in Scotland? Was this stability a desirable condition for the people of Scotland (explore this fully, there are several sides to the question)?

3   What was the major single challenge to this stability?

4   What part did the Scots play in the Restoration of the monarchy?

Specimen Answer and   1   (a) The army of those Presbyterians who had done a deal with
Discussion   Charles II; (b) the army of the Presbyterian Remonstrants or Protesters, opposed to Charles; (c) the Royalist army in the Highlands; (d) Cromwell's army. Cromwell's army won.

2   In the sense that Scotland was conquered and united with England. Few Scots can have been very happy with such a situation. Economically the union was operated entirely to England's advantage. By encouraging the Protesters, the English ensured that the unfortunate split in the Scottish kirk would be perpetuated. But justice was improved, and life was more secure.

Figure 32
William Dobson, Charles II
when Prince of Wales with
page, *undated, oil on
canvas, 156.6 x 129.8 cm.
Scottish National Portrait
Gallery.*

3   Glencairn's Rising. (I'll discuss this more fully later.)

4   Not a big one, save that, in remaining at peace after the withdrawal of Monck's army (in itself a sign that stability had been quite firmly established) they helped to make possible the developments which led to the Restoration.

Ireland to 1660

Before summarizing the main developments I want you to work through the following exercise which will help you to relate what you already know to this unit.

Exercise   1   You have just seen how stability was brought to Scotland. Now think about the differences between Ireland and Scotland at the beginning of our period, particularly with regard to the prospects for the imposition of stable English rule. How did Ireland differ from Scotland in regard (a) to geography and (b) to population (origins, religion, in particular, perhaps also something on politics and social status)?

2   Why were English military operations likely to be more brutal in Ireland than in Scotland?

Specimen Answers and   1   (a) Scotland is contiguous with England: English armies and
Discussion   administrators had to get across the Irish sea. Coward (p.248) also refers to the 'fate of earlier English armies in the bogs of Ireland'. The first point is more relevant as there were bogs in Scotland too. It had considerable ramifications: even when Ireland was governed directly from England, there had to be, because of the geographical problem, a local executive in Dublin. This executive would be bound to give weight to local conditions as it perceived them, which might well result in differences with Whitehall. (b) While Scotland was relatively homogeneous (the sharpness and significance of the divide between Highlands and Lowlands is often exaggerated), Ireland was divided sharply into different religious communities and interest groups – making the imposition of unity and stability difficult.

Communities and interest groups

Seventeenth-century Ireland contained a number of different communities. The following is a synopsis of the various interest groups found there during this period.

1   Gaelic Irish Catholics, landowners and merchants as well as peasants and landless labourers.

2   Old English, Catholic descendants of the medieval English settlers, many of them landowners and merchants.

3   English and Scots settlers, Anglicans and Presbyterians, who arrived in the late sixteenth and early seventeenth centuries and were settled in the plantations especially in Munster and Ulster (see the map in Coward, p.126, and Fig. 20, above). Many of these English settlers supported the king.

4   Adventurers, English speculators who advanced money to the English government from 1642 onwards in return for allocations of land in Ireland. Few ever went to Ireland.

5   Cromwellian soldiers, paid for their service in Ireland from 1649 in debentures issued on Irish land. Many of them sold their debentures for cash and returned to England. Soldiers were responsible for the appearance of the first Baptist, Quaker and Independent sectarian congregations in Ireland.

The alliances and rivalries between these groups did not conduce to stability, and sometimes divided the executive in Dublin.

To many English people Catholicism was synonymous with perfidy and bloodshed and Coward (p.248) quotes effectively from the writings of Oliver Cromwell: 'I had rather be overrun with a Cavalierish interest, than a Scotch interest; I had rather be overrun with a Scotch interest, than an Irish interest; and I think of all this is the most dangerous ... all the world knows their barbarism'.

Now for my summary of the four main phases in Irish government, from the end of the civil war to 1660.

Summary of developments

The Re-conquest of Ireland, 1649–52

You will have learnt something about this in Unit 3. The royalist leader in Ireland was the Protestant landowner, the Earl of Ormonde. However, another Protestant landowner, Lord Broghill, accepted a command in Cromwell's army. Ormonde suffered a serious defeat just before Cromwell arrived in August 1649, aiming to destroy support for the king, and also to subdue the Roman Catholics (who did not necessarily support the king). Cromwell left in May 1650, being succeeded as Commander-in-Chief by Ireton. While Ireton's successor, Fleetwood, was travelling out in early 1652, Ludlow effectively completed the conquest with the capture of Galway.

The New Settlement, 1652–4

The Irish land settlement had been planned by the Long Parliament, but was modified and extended, particularly with regard to finding land for soldiers, by the Acts of Settlement (Rump, August 1652) and of Satisfaction (Barebones Parliament, September 1653). The Catholics were declared rebels, the better to confiscate their land: from 59 per cent in

Figure 33 (opposite)
Land debenture, 1658, reproduced from J. Prendergast, The Cromwellian Settlement of Ireland, *1870 (enlarged editions) London, Longmans, Green, Reader and Dyer.*

By the Commissioners appointed for Stateing the
Arreares of the Souldiery And of Publique faith
Debts in Ireland /

UPon Composition and Agreement made with *Mrs Ester Hunt Administratrix to her late Husband Capt Thomas Hunt Deceased in behalfe of her selfe And for those of Henry Thomas Beniamin Anne Hester and Sarah Hunt Children of the said Defunct* for *all the said Defuncts* ——— Arrears for Service in *Ireland* from the *Last Day of December* 1646 *to the 5th Day of June* 1649 *As Capt of a troope of Horse in Coll Chudley Cootes Regiment*

£ 718
714, 17 06

There remains due from the Common-wealth to the *said Ester Hunt and y said Children of the defunct theire* Executors, Administrators, or Assign's, the Sum of *Seaven hundred and fowerteene Pounds Seaventeene Shillings and Sixpence* —— which is to be satisfied to the said *Ester Hunt and y said Children of y Defunct theire* Executors, Administrators, or Assign's, out of the Rebels Lands, Houses, Tenements and Hereditaments in *Ireland*; or other Lands, Houses, Tenements and Hereditaments there, in the dispose of the *Common-wealth* of ENGLAND. Signed and Sealed at DUBLIN the *Six and twentieth* day of *May* —— 1658

Examined and entred

Tho Herbert
Son Register

Edw Roberts
Robert Gorges
Rob Jefferys

1641, the Catholic share of land fell to 20 per cent in 1660, the bulk of which was in Connaught. Thus far Ireland was being governed by parliamentary commissioners sent out from Westminster, and under the authority of the Commander-in-Chief. In August 1654, Cromwell decided to revive the post of Lord Deputy, and institute a council to assist him.

Fleetwood, a rather weak man, hater of Catholics, hostile to Anglican settlers, unfriendly to Presbyterians, but a warm upholder of the sectaries, remained in power, since the new title was conferred on him. Meantime it was decided (by the Instrument of Government) that Ireland would send thirty MPs to Westminster.

The rule of Henry Cromwell, 1655–9

Cromwell's son served with him in Ireland in 1650. On 25 December 1654 he was appointed major-general and acting commander of the forces in Ireland, and also a member of the Irish Council, though he delayed his return to Ireland till July 1655. Fleetwood had favoured the religious radicals; Henry Cromwell hoped to give fair weight to all interests, then, finding most conflicts irreconcilable, decided that the only hope of achieving stability lay in cultivating the Protestant settlers. Fleetwood returned to England, yet retained the title of Lord Deputy, and was thus able to continue, along with several members of the Council, to contest the policies favoured by Henry Cromwell. When his commission expired in September 1657, Oliver Cromwell left the post vacant for two months (such was the conflict of opinion as to which interests should be allowed to predominate) before finally settling it on Henry Cromwell. Only now could the latter fulfil his policy of granting more land and power to the English settlers. A new balance of power (the foundation of the later Protestant Ascendancy) was established. While not in any way challenging the land settlement as it affected Catholics, Henry did try to mitigate the imposition of the Oath of Abjuration (1657), aimed at forcing Catholics to deny Catholic doctrine and the authority of the pope. In November 1658, success seemed crowned when Richard Cromwell named his brother Lord Lieutenant and governor-general.

Turmoil, 1659–60

The fall of Richard Cromwell brought Henry's dismissal in June 1659. The various groups briefly in power in England attempted a return to government by parliamentary commissioners. However, English settlers, now greatly strengthened thanks to the policies of Henry Cromwell, first seized Dublin Castle (13 December 1659), then set up a General Convention which acted as an Irish parliament. But once the Restoration in England became inevitable, there was little the Convention could do but acquiesce.

Outline of developments and trends, France 1653–69

First read Briggs (pp. 134–42), then Offprint 9.

Exercise 1 From your reading of both texts comment on the significance of the following dates as representing steps towards restoration of stability: 1653 1655 1657 1659 1661 1662 1665 1669.

2 List the main challenges to the regime mentioned by Briggs (also use the map on p.115). Where possible note the social status of the protesters or rebels. Is it possible to make a generalization about the social status of the opposition to the regime?

3 With respect to the restoration of stability how do the actions of the monarchy in this period differ critically from those in the 1630s?

4 (a) How would you describe the attitude of Dessert and Journet towards Colbert? (b) What is the major historical point they are making?

Specimen Answers and 1 1653. Briggs has selected this date as the one marking 'the
Discussion restoration of royal control over France'. He might have chosen 1652, the year, as you already know, of the recall (in October) of Mazarin. However, it was not till the late summer of 1653 (Briggs, p.132) that the rebels in Bordeaux surrendered.

1655. This is the date at which the tax-gathering system (vital to royal power) was operating again much as it had before the Frondes.

1657. The stalemate in the war with Spain was undoubtedly sapping royal power, so that the alliance with England of this year (remember the praise for Cromwell's foreign policy) did provide immense relief.

1659. The Peace of the Pyrenees. If we wanted to underline the influence of foreign policy on domestic developments, then we might well single out this as marking an important stage in, in particular, limiting (for the time being) the expenses of the crown.

1661. This, surely, is an important step. I'm sure you noted what Dessert and Journet say in their very first sentence; and Briggs begins a whole new section with it. No more Mazarins; the king is assuming direct personal rule.

1662. This (Briggs, foot of p.141) is when, for the first time, a batch of taxation arrears was officially written off. Formally, this was in celebration of the birth of the dauphin (and hearty congratulations if you singled that out, since the birth of a male heir was seen as a guarantee of future stability – though that is not the main issue here), but in fact it was an important advance in financial management.

1665. Two events in this year highlight the eminence of Colbert. He is appointed Controller General, and he founds the Academy of Sciences. We could take this date as registering the completion of Colbert's financial reforms.

1669. 'The Peace of the Church'. As this brought the continuing religious conflicts within the French Catholic church (see below, pp. 147–8) to an end it does mark an important stage.

2   (a) Angers, 1656: tax revolt by 'lesser bourgeoisie' (i.e. shopkeepers, small-scale manufacturers of, for example, furniture, or medicines, owners of stables, etc.).

(b)   Protests of local nobles in several western provinces, 1658.

(c)   Peasant revolt in the Sologne, 1658.

(d)   Dangerous faction struggle in Marseille (meaning a struggle between different groups of civic leaders, of the Marseille bourgeoisie), 1658.

(e)   Persistent trouble in the south west, especially Saintonge and Angoumois, in the late 1650s. (It's not made clear for you, but these involved all levels of local society.)

(f)   Disorder in Provence, and uprising in Aix (the provincial capital), 1659. (In fact, all levels of society were involved, most especially local noble and bourgeois leaders.)

(g)   1659–60: Continuing trouble in Provence and in its major port, Marseille, mainly involving local leaders. (You may feel that the way in which this revolt was crushed marks a stage in the growth of royal control, and indeed may have included this in the previous exercise. All credit to you if you did, though I incline to the view that if a king has to lead an army into his own territory, that is actually a sign of considerable instability.)

(h)   Revolt of peasants in the Boulonnais, 1662.

(i)   Revolt in the Pyrenees under popular leader Audijos. (The revolt took place in 1664 and was very much a revolt of ordinary people – against the special Bordeaux wine-tax.)

That actually brings us up to the end of our period, though you will have noted that revolts did continue – so stability was far from completely assured in 1669. On the social status of protesters and rebels clearly it varied; sometimes all classes were involved, sometimes only one.

3   Royal actions against threats or potential threats are vigorous and severe.

4   (a) They seem rather hostile to him. This is what might be called a 'debunking' article. They speak of 'his odious and lying attacks on Fouquet'.

(b)   The main historical point is that Colbert was very much a man of his time, the product of a particular economic and political system. He derived great benefits from his family background and contacts, and he deliberately followed the sort of apprenticeship which would lead to his being a top financier. His success as the king's chief finance minister was based on the 'clan' that he had so assiduously built up (Offprint 9, p.55).

Challenges to authority: British Isles 1649–60, France, 1653–69

You should now have in mind a clear framework of events and some preliminary thoughts about the problems involved in, and the extent of, the re-establishment of stability. You should start reflecting on what you have learned about the main issues, or areas of contention giving rise to challenges to the central government.

We shall now examine the main issues or areas of contention giving rise to challenges to central authority.

Types of challenge

Finance

Clearly taxation is a constant bone of contention: governments constantly needed revenue. Another way governments could raise money was by seizing land then, usually selling it off, or handing it over to those who had already put up funds. Seizures (ostensibly as a punishment) and fines inevitably provoked opposition. However, taxation caused almost continuous resentment among practically all classes.

Religion

Religion was a prime incentive for people to harass and torture each other, and to resist governments which insisted upon the supremacy of one particular church.

'General lawlessness'

This covers those criminal activities which, without specific political or religious motivation, go on in a violent and little-policed society. These can, self-evidently, be a direct threat to stability; also, perhaps more seriously, a government which fails to provide security can become dangerously unpopular. (Fleetwood lost favour because of his inability to control the various factions in Ireland; the Restoration came about in England because after the death of Oliver Cromwell no republican or army grouping was capable of providing security.)

The political dimension

Finally there is the political dimension, open opposition or revolt. We can, perhaps, postulate three levels of intensity: discontent, quite likely over taxation or other economic matters; protest; and revolt – the latter two taking us into the political, and, indeed military, domain. In our studies so far we have encountered two different levels of upheaval: (a) one aimed at changing the entire regime and form of government; (b) the other concerned with the local disposition of power or with the way the central authority is administered locally, taxes collected, etc. As we have seen, one of these levels was more prevalent in the British Isles, the other more prevalent in France.

Exercise   1   Think about the two different levels of revolt referred to above. Which was more prevalent in the British Isles and which in France?

2   Where did taxation meet with most dangerous resistance?

Specimen Answers and   1   In the British Isles the royalist uprisings aimed at overthrowing
Discussion   republican government and restoring the monarchy, changing the entire regime. In France Condé, aided till 1659 by Spain, may have hoped to secure the crown for himself, but there was no thought of overthrowing the institution of the monarchy. But there was in France a great deal of local discontent – from Briggs you compiled an extensive list of local uprisings.

2   France: many of these very uprisings were related to the tax issue. There was discontent over taxation in all parts of the British Isles, and objections to the increased taxation under the rule of the major–generals did much to make the second Protectorate Parliament uncooperative, but there was no armed resistance to taxation.

Having thought about some of the underlying factors concerning challenges to authority we shall now look at six actual examples.

'Glencairn's Rising', 1653–4

The traditional label for this complex and confusing episode in Scottish history is misleading. The 'rising' was both less and more than the term suggests. It was no sharp, sudden blow to the English authority established by Cromwell's conquest, but more a species of guerrilla war. The Earl of Glencairn was scarcely more than nominal leader, formally acting for Charles II's Commander-in-Chief for Scotland, Lieutenant-General (later Earl of) Middleton (who was on the continent trying to raise funds for the royalist cause), but beset by rivals who eventually edged him out (so that Glencairn ended up leading a faction detached from the main body of Scottish royalist forces). The rising began and ended in the Highlands, but Glencairn himself was a Lowlander, as was his principal rival in the royalist camp, the Earl of Balcarres.

Scotland was a wretchedly poor country in which ordinary thievery and murder were endemic; conditions were worst in the Highlands where the land simply could not support the population, and where mechanisms of local government were poorly developed. Added to this were the perennial clan feuds, whose origins lay deep in the past. Misery, discontent, and ordinary lawlessness (throughout Scotland) merged into nationalistic resentment at English rule, and all of this found a focal point in royalist rebellion. As Dow (1979, p.75), has pointed out, royalism, at this particular time, actually made a better vehicle for national sentiment than rigid, covenanting Presbyterianism. Most support, particularly in the Lowlands, was passive rather than active: what later generations, in fact, would recognize as the classic guerrilla war situation, vexing and difficult for the English.

From December 1652 the English army of occupation in Scotland was commanded by Colonel Robert Lilburne, not only a relatively junior figure, but also a tense and sensitive one. Within a month news was coming through of stirrings of military rebellion in both Ayrshire and the Highlands, the latter being attributed to economic circumstances – only by despoiling others could the Highlanders subsist. It was reported also that a royalist agent had landed in Fife and sped off to the Highlands. By June/July a state of 'full-scale military revolt' (Dow, 1979, p.80) had been reached, with Glencairn designated acting commander by Charles. In autumn the royalists mounted lightning raids into the Lowlands, penetrating, in late November, as far south as Galloway and Carlisle. In late March there were local risings in Dumfries and Galloway. There were few set-pieces battles; those that there were won by the English. But the 'jack-in-the-box quality of the insurrection' (Dow, 1979, p.86) made it very difficult to deal with: no sooner did the English triumph in one place than insurrections broke out in two or three others. For considerable periods the royalists were able to impose taxes on the lands they occupied. At their best they were more moderate in their demands than the Cromwellian tax-gatherers; and indeed efforts were made to present the outlines of a broad coalition against the English rather than a too narrowly royalist ideology. Lilburne was constantly stretched, and frequently feared the worst: in December, he reported to Cromwell that 'people almost universally have a kind of muttering and expectation of some change'.

For all that, the insurrection had many weaknesses. At no time was there freedom from internal clan feuding; many leaders were most concerned with striking the best bargains for themselves; several areas remained indifferent or hostile; too much faith was put in the likelihood of support from a Dutch invasion. The safety and security brought by English rule worked against the rebels, though more efficient prosecution of debts hit the lesser gentry and forced many of them towards the royalist cause. After the Highland incursions the citizens of Moray and Nairn welcomed the English soldiers, referring to the 'great swearings, cursings, drinkings, whoorings of that Highland crew'. The Perthshire gentry gave as their reason for not joining the rising that they had 'had too large a share in the former sufferings for the King; and now having engaged to live peaceably, and give submission to the union, they will rather lose their crops than their inheritance'.

But what is most important in assessing the significance of 'Glencairn's Rising' is that the English, in facing what, for a time, did appear as a serious menace to the regime in Scotland, were forced to make concessions. From the early summer of 1653, many of the nobility and gentry were given the right to bear arms, while whole localities were permitted to raise armed guards, the better to combat both royalist depredations and ordinary lawlessness; the army, in effect, was sharing power with the people. By the time Monck took over from Lilburne in April 1654, the insurrection was well past its peak. But Monck continued, and extended, Lilburne's policies. Relief was granted to those gentry who found it so impossible to pay off their debts; reductions were made in tax assessments and property valuations; most important of all a strong element of clemency was introduced in mitigation of those most grievously resented impositions on royalists and suspected royalists, fines and sequestrations. Finally, (as a product, however, of English political developments as well as Scottish ones) the establishment in September 1655 of a Council in Scotland marked a move away from military to civilian government (though, as we have noted before, Cromwellian government did continue, in the last analysis, to depend on the army).

There is, as is well known, another side to Monck's policies. To him the insurrection was still heavy with menace (even if, in reality, it was now a bit of a shambles). On 9 June 1654 he embarked on his march of pillage and destruction through the Highlands, partly aimed at making it impossible for that region again to sustain a rebellion, and partly at capturing Middleton who had at last landed in Scotland earlier in the year. Monck was still pursuing the elusive Middleton in March 1655, when his anxieties were sharply increased by the news of Penruddock's Rising in Wiltshire and Dorset. Middleton, it may be noted, eventually escaped back to the continent. Meantime 'Glencairn's Rising' had sunk back whence it had come, into the turbulent waters of Highland lawlessness – which Monck continued to perceive as a potential threat to stability right up to his involvement in the train of events which brought the Restoration.

Penruddock's Rising, March 1655
Glencairn's Rising kept the English forces in Scotland stretched and guessing for a full eighteen months, but was essentially the product of a conjunction of specifically Scottish circumstances, though, of course, it did have strong formal contact with royalist strategists abroad. Penruddock's Rising began after dark on Sunday 11 March, and was all over by late afternoon the following Wednesday, but was part of a concerted royalist plan involving insurrections all over England, though, in the event it did reveal some specific local characteristics. The upshot of the Scottish episode was a softening of English attitudes towards the Scottish political nation; that of the English one the imposition of the harsh and unpopular rule of the major–generals. Glencairn exposed the weaknesses in the English hold on Scotland; Penruddock revealed the fundamental strengths of the Cromwellian regime, not least Thurloe's intelligence system, but also the degree of popular support it enjoyed.

The rising was part of a nation-wide conspiracy, yet it drew upon local sentiment, and was supported by many very humble people. In drawing up a list of 139 rebels, Desborough deliberately excluded many 'of the meaner sort', yet that list contained only 43 gentlemen, together with 8 yeomen, 19 husbandmen, 10 servants, 2 innkeepers, with most of the remaining 57 being small craftsmen or traders. Underdown (1987, p.236) notes that the rising embodied 'a protest by the 'Country' against the intrusions of a Puritan central government' and 'a strong popular nostalgia for the imagined good old days of neighbourliness and fellowship'.

Booth's Rebellion, August 1659
There followed the rule of the eleven major–generals (Desborough assumed full, as distinct from emergency, powers on 28 May) and the hated decimation tax, imposed on all royalist sympathizers (see Coward, p.270). In Charles's circle abroad, and in the clandestine Sealed Knot in England, plots continued to be hatched. With the death of Oliver, the possibility was envisaged of a national rising involving royalists and Presbyterians. The leader in Cheshire was to be the Presbyterian, Sir George Booth. Once again, despite the disintegration of the Protectorate, the

national rising, intended for 1 August 1659, was a fiasco, though Booth and his supporters (particularly Colonel Ireland) did have some remarkable initial successes, effectively taking control of most of Lancashire and Cheshire, mustering combined forces of around 4,000. But under Generals Lambert and Ludlow the central army was too strong for them. Well before the end of August the revolt was over, and Booth, fleeing as 'Lady Dorothy' was arrested at a Newport Pagnell inn after asking for a barber. For all the uncertainties of 1659 the framework of government was still very solid: because there was no acceptable individual or group to head that framework, the way was opening to an orderly restoration of monarchy, but not to conspiracy and violent upheaval.

The Languedoc Revolt of 1655–7

We are going to approach this important event through a brief excerpt from one single source (*Anthology*, I.21). If we're going to make any use of a brief excerpt we'll need to know a bit about what is in the rest of the document as well as about its nature and origins, and a bit about the historical context of the document. I'm going to provide you with that, and then I'm going to go on and work through the document, for once doing all the work myself, in order to prepare you for the exercise which follows, where we look at a different episode, and a clutch of brief documents relating to it.

Languedoc was one of the French provinces with its own Estates – the assembly of nobles, clergy and commoners. The immediate cause of the crisis was the winter quartering in the province of the royal army, the army engaged in Catalonia against the Spaniards. A session of the Estates had just opened and the royal commissioners were demanding 2,250,000 livres in order to pay these soldiers. The Estates were determined that no such levy could be exacted without their express consent. But, worse than that, the troops were already receiving free board and lodging at the expense of the local communities. The Estates were terrified that the communities would be forced into paying out cash to the troops, raised by injudicious borrowing, thus threatening financial chaos, while at the same time infringing the Estates' control of all fiscal arrangements within the province. During the Frondes the province's successful opposition to the royal government had been expressed through a union between the Estates and the Toulouse *parlement*. The Estates now sought to revive that union by sending deputies to the *parlement*, requesting that it issue a decree prohibiting the communities from borrowing money. The *parlement* did as asked, and so, with the union apparently in operation again, the Estates announced that the troops must be withdrawn, then they would, by their own decision, make a monetary grant to the king. Their case was put directly to Mazarin by their representative in Paris, Baron de Lanta. The arguments in *Anthology*, I.21 may be dishonest or ill-founded, but we can take it that the report of them is, in essence, accurate since an inaccurate report would have been useless both for Lanta and the Estates.

Now read through *Anthology*, I.21 once or twice, to get the main drift, then keep referring to it as I give my comments.

We see in the first paragraph that Mazarin does not refer to the traditional rights Lanta had been claiming. Instead he pressurizes Lanta by selecting issues which amount to accusing the Estates of conspiracy, and by expressing the king's extreme anger over this (a not very subtle threat). The first issue is the revival of the union between Estates and *parlement*, which had been such a potent weapon against the monarchy during the Frondes. The king and Mazarin, of course, are determined at all costs to avoid a repetition of the Frondes: when they say that the times of unions are over, they meant that the Frondes, and all the anti-government conspiracies that went with it, are over. The second issue is that the Estates had been scheming to ruin the troops, so that they would never be quartered in Languedoc again. The proof, says Mazarin, lies in the decrees, requested of the *parlement* by the Estates, prohibiting the communities from borrowing money. The final phrase is again a threat, reminding Lanta that he is no longer dealing with a weak regency government as in the Frondes.

Lanta denies that there were any plots against the troops and he tries to minimize the significance of the delegation to the *parlement* by saying that it was going in any case to thank the *parlement* for previous favours (*liards* were small copper coins minted for the poor to use, but very unpopular since richer people often refused to accept them; the draining of marshes was another regular grievance of ordinary people who lived off their produce). Lanta makes it sound as if the decree about borrowing was merely a kind of after-thought. Nevertheless, he does go on to make a substantive defence of the decree. Rash borrowing by the communities in the past had caused great misery (the war of Privas was a Protestant uprising which for several months in 1653 threatened a resumption of full-scale religious war); furthermore such decrees had been issued by the (king's) council itself. The accusation of forming a union is obviously the one which bites deepest; Lanta denies that there had ever been any such intention, unions indeed being obnoxious to the Estates. But, he says, moving back now onto the attack, some unions come about naturally. This one, though he agrees it would be wrong (against 'liberty') to declare it officially and openly, was forced by the government's own attacks on two worthy bodies, the Estates and the *parlement*. He ends on a conciliatory note. If the traditional rights of the province (this had been the basic point from the start) are safeguarded, and if (here he is throwing in a completely new point) the threat to the *parlement* at Toulouse, through the creation of a new one at Nîmes, is withdrawn, peace will be restored. While such discussion was going on in Paris, there was a good deal of unrest and mounting violence in Languedoc itself. In late December there were serious incidents, resulting in five killed, as the *parlement*'s commissioner was trying to rally local peasants against an undisciplined regiment. Yet the significance of this document is that it reveals the constraints within which, in the true seats of power, the debate was conducted. Lanta was desperate to avoid charges of conspiracy and basically all he was fighting for was a formal recognition of traditional privileges. The Estates granted two million livres, provided illegal exactions already made were subtracted; they then agreed to a further levy provided proper receipts were issued.

Although ordinary people were inevitably involved, this episode was very much provoked by the provincial aristocracy, concerned with local privileges. While, in formal terms, they managed to preserve face, what was clearly revealed was that the reality of power was now very much with the central government, which, in fact, succeeded in getting all of its financial requirements. Beik (1985, p.215) refers to these events as an echo of the Frondes but, now that the balance of power has swung back towards the monarchy, they are not nearly so serious. Remember, however, that this was only one of many episodes which beset the government in the 1650s (and this is not actually one of the ones mentioned by Briggs).

The Revolt in the Boulonnais, 1662

Anthology, I.22A–G comprise a series of letters from Machault, Special Royal Commissioner in the Boulonnais to Colbert, together with two official documents of record. From these it is possible to piece together quite a full account of events which are quite typical of the 'popular' revolts of the 1650s (this one is listed by Briggs). The revolt had the tacit support of the local aristocracy, though there was bitter hostility between the peasant rebels and some of the lesser nobility and bourgeoisie; that the leader was a minor noble just drives home the complexity of history. The Boulonnais is the region forming the hinterland of the important port of Boulogne, and is itself part of the province of Picardy. It was a custom of Louis, when making a tax demand, to present it as if he was actually making a gracious concession. Remember also how jealous the provinces were of their historic privileges.

Exercise Read all of *Anthology,* I.22. Then go back and write down comments on each extract, saying what it tells us about the developing situation, while also assessing the reliability of the document and commenting upon any significant, or obscure, words and phrases.

Specimen Answer and *Anthology,* I.22A. This is a formal record of the Council of State and thus,
Discussion although the wishes of the king, as expressed here, may be utterly hypocritical, the document itself is an accurate record of them. We learn that the Boulonnais (as the hinterland to a major military port) has suffered heavy damage in the recent wars (against Spain). What the king wants is a levy of 30,000 livres which he presents as a reduction representing 'the fruits of peace', though actually, as we learn from the next document, he had no right to demand this in time of peace. The 'taxable subjects' in the Boulonnais, as we also learn from the next document, are simply 'the ordinary people'. Collecting tax through the *intendant* (who usually doubled as *Maître des Requêtes* at the Court – see Glossary in Briggs) had been the standard royal practice before the Frondes; here we have unwitting testimony that the system is back in full operation. Finally, one might comment on the characteristic arrogance manifested by Louis when he talks of the peace (of the Pyrenees, of course) 'He has just procured for the whole of Europe'. (I hope this gives you a clear idea of the range of comments that can usefully be made going beyond the mundane task of simply paraphrasing the document: if you feel you would like to go back and improve your other answers, please do so now.)

Anthology, I.22B. It is a year later; as a result of the intentions expressed in the previous document, revolt has broken out. Evidently Machault has been sent out to investigate and take appropriate action. This is his first report (it is unwitting testimony to the importance of Colbert that the letters are all addressed to him). Colbert wants the facts; it's Machault's duty to provide them: we'll find arrogance and snobbery, no doubt, but on the whole we can expect these letters to be accurate. This impression is confirmed by the way he spells out the history of the privileges of the Boulonnais, something, certainly, the government would prefer not to hear about, particularly the bit about the tax being illegal in time of peace. It is this tax, falling exclusively on the ordinary people, which has caused the revolt. Quite clearly, from this account, it is the people who have revolted, 'the flame' spreading 'from village to village', that is, it is not just a minority who are involved. Though the phrasing may be snobbish, the joining in of vagabonds and layabouts (who would be unlikely to be taxpayers, but who would hope to profit from the disturbances) was pretty usual. Unions between people of very different social status in such revolts was also quite usual: here, we learn, the nobles are supporting the rebels. Although taxation does not affect them, they would be keen anyway to defend provincial privileges (as in Languedoc).

Anthology, I.22C. The fact that Machault is collecting eye-witness reports further supports the general reliability of his letters. Here we do have evidence of social divisions: 'men of noble birth' (by which is meant lesser nobles), as well as bourgeois figures, have been attacked by the peasantry for not supporting them.

Anthology, I.22D. This letter tells us of the suppression of the revolt (which, we can see from the dates of the letters has lasted about two months). Evidently, against assembled troops, there was little the rebels could do, hence their unconditional surrender. The notions of 'justice' of this stage in Louis XIV's reign (earlier revolts – part of earlier instability – had been treated quite leniently) come through strongly: summary hangings, the galleys for several hundred. (Comparisons with England are instructive here: after Penruddock's rising Cromwell had insisted on trial by jury; there were no English galley ships, though we mustn't forget that prisoners were transported as indentured servants to Barbados – still nothing like as awful as being in the galleys). Machault may be exhibiting a qualm of conscience when he remarks of the hangings that they 'are customary on such occasions', though that simply further confirms the harshness of the regime. He goes on to exult that there is nothing to do now but raise the 30,000 livres, and probably an additional tax as well. The government is winning hands down. Saint-Pouanges (second cousin to Colbert), incidentally, had replaced d'Ormesson as *intendant*.

Anthology, I.22E. This letter encloses Machault's judgements so far. From the letter itself one can see that the objective is stability through terror. The 'pyramids' mentioned in the judgement, to be erected at the centres of revolt, are to serve, as it were, as propaganda on behalf of royal 'justice' and power. That the revolt is perceived as one ultimately involving all classes is seen in the way the ban on arms and assembly applies to all classes. Taken in conjunction with the one-year removal of the bells and restrictions on trading and markets in the two leading villages, it becomes clear that the deeper objective is to inflict humiliation on civic pride.

Anthology, I.22F. Unwittingly this letter conveys the information that the leader was actually of the (minor) nobility. The judgement details the horrific death he is to suffer. Again the spreading of fear is the obvious motivation.

Anthology, I.22G. Machault had dealt with the leaders. Here we have the official record of the Council decisions about what was to be done with the rest. Perhaps there is a touch of mercy in the releasing of the under-twenty-ones, and over sixty-nines. The 400 fittest are to be selected for the galleys (for ever) showing a revealing mixing of 'justice' with the needs of the navy. (A further document, which I have not included, tells us that even when the 400 were selected many were so feeble that they looked likely to die before ever they reached the ships – an illuminating comment on the health and nutrition of the French poor of the time.)

The Religious Fronde and Jansenism

You will already be aware of the conflicts and cross-currents created in the British Isles by religious faith: the radical sects detested Cromwellian compromise and strove to influence events in Ireland, where the Protestant/Catholic divide was a bitter one; in Scotland there were at least two sorts of Presbyterian; Anglicans supported royalist conspiracies. Let me, therefore, turn to France.

Golden (1981, p.3) has claimed that 'there was a third Fronde, the Religious Fronde, which lasted from 1652 to 1662 and whose major participants were the Parisian *curés*, the parish priests charged with the care of souls and with penitential discipline'. What the *curés* wanted was complete control over their parishes, and in this struggle they supported the archbishop of Paris, the Cardinal de Retz, and thus were drawn into direct opposition to the king, an opposition made still more bitter by the *curés'* espousal of Richerism and Jansenism (you'll find this explained in a moment when you read a few pages of Briggs). As Golden (1981, p.3) notes: 'The years after 1652–53 were marked by violence'. And he sums up his argument thus:

> Because Retz was already the leader of a faction, because the government faced other serious problems throughout the decade (primarily the war against Spain and the recurrent financial crisis), because of his support by the *curés*, and because of the increasing ecclesiastical importance of Paris, his opposition threatened the ministeriat [i.e. government]. One aspect of the Religious Fronde was therefore political, consisting of the struggle to control Paris. (Golden, 1981, p.14)

Finally, Golden makes the crucially important point that: 'The crown feared that at any time the *curés*, through their control of the pulpit, could incite their parishioners to open rebellion ...' (p.152).

Now, to get a wider perspective on all that, I want you to turn to Briggs, p.176, starting at the section 'The Jansenist quarrel' and read through to the middle of p.181, '... from 1669 Jansenists were no longer openly persecuted, although the authorities discriminated against them whenever possible'.

Exercise　1　Note down and, as necessary, explain briefly, the main elements making for dissension and conflict. You can then compare your list with mine.

2　Try to assess the seriousness of this religious dissension and conflict as direct challenge to government authority; also ask yourself whether from this point of view religious conflict was more serious in France or in the British Isles.

These are questions on which I myself find great difficulty in coming to firm conclusions. If you feel confident enough write down your own answers; if not, at least ponder the issues, then wait for my discussion.

Specimen Answer and Discussion

1 (a)   Uncertainty among the faithful as to what direction the Catholic Reformation should now take, leading to deepening quarrels among the devout.

(b)   Spread of Jansenism, a predestinarian brand of Catholicism, characterized by certainty, moral fervour, and the pushing of arguments to logical extremes. Hostility to the government was one of its most enduring characteristics.

(c)   The bitter clash between Jansenists and Jesuits, who were strong in Rome and at court. The Jesuits, master of 'organization, intrigue and publicity', took aggressive action against the Jansenists (e.g. nuns of Port Royale; Arnault at Sorbonne).

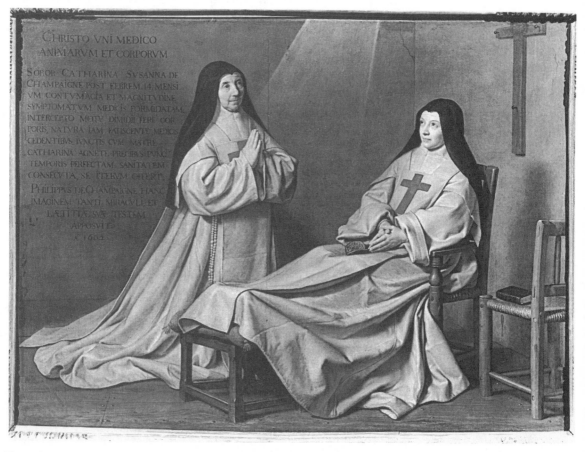

Figure 34
Philippe de Champaigne, Mother Catherine- Agnès Arnauld and Sister Catherine de Sainte Suzanne Champaigne (niece of painter), two nuns of Port Royal, *1662, oil on canvas, 165 x 229 cm. Musée du Louvre Photo: Photo: Réunion des Musées Nationaux Documentation Photographique.*

(d) The Jansenists had solid support among the Paris élites, particularly the *noblesse de robe*. The small group of Jansenist bishops was 'a painful thorn in the government's side'. Louis XIV was a bitter enemy, imprisoning and exiling them (this coming to an end with the Peace of the Church, 1669).

2 Personally, I think Golden, like many scholars who have produced highly original new work, exaggerates the significance of his 'Religious Fronde', and indeed that the term 'fronde' is scarcely justified (it is because of my disagreement with Golden, incidentally, that I thought it best to quote directly his own words). It seems to me that the significance of religion in all four countries was that it created an almost permanent condition of potential conflict at all levels of society, but that, because of the strength of the various governments, it never had the opportunity of, in itself, mounting a direct challenge to central authority. In France there were no serious Protestant challenges after 1629, but I would none the less conclude that, given the very sharp split with Catholicism, religion in France was just as significant as a potential destabilizing factor as it was in the British Isles. In the upshot, there was no revolt founded basically, or mainly, on religion (Booth's rebellion was primarily in the royalist cause, though it did seek to join Presbyterians and Anglicans).

Consequences

Working out the consequences of great events such as the civil wars or the Frondes can never be simple nor exact. Because there were constitutional experiments, as well as social changes, in the period we are studying, that does not necessarily mean that they were caused by these events. With or without great events, other forces in history continue in operation. And, of course, there were all sorts of new events and developments in our period, which themselves had 'consequences'. In this section I am simply going to pick out the main developments affecting (a) princes, and (b) peoples, which were the consequences both of the big upheavals and of what happened in their aftermath.

Constitutional consequences

In the Frondes royal power faced a strong challenge; in the civil war it was wiped out. Thus in the British Isles there had to be constitutional innovation, while in France there had at least to be renovation. Since civil war and then military conquest extended into Scotland and Ireland new constitutional arrangements had to be established between the three countries.

You already know the outline of major developments. Here we are simply going to look at three documents (*Anthology*, I.23–25) I have chosen relating mainly (though not exclusively) to constitutional issues. I want you now to read these carefully in conjunction with the following comments:

Anthology, I.23. Although the Union came about by virtue of Cromwell's conquest of Scotland, note (first paragraph) that it is maintained that Scottish assent has been obtained, and, more critically, that Scotland is being treated as an independent consenting party to a mutual agreement (Ireland was treated differently, there being no Ordinance of Union, even though the Irish parliament, also, disappeared). There are to be thirty Scottish MPs (this simply confirms the Instrument of Government, which gave the same ration to Ireland, and 400 to England). In practice many of the MPs were English soldiers or officials rather than genuine Scottish representatives. No longer were there to be any customs and excise duties as between Scotland and England (second paragraph), but England's external duties were to apply to Scotland which, as you already know from Mitchison, was very much to Scotland's disadvantage. 'Proportionable' taxation (final paragraph) would fall heavily on a poor country like Scotland, but, as we saw in discussing Glencairn's Rising, there were modifications; Ireland was taxed more severely than Scotland. Taken together these points indicate the document's historical significance in demonstrating Scotland's constitutional position within the Cromwellian union.

Anthology, I.24. The Humble Petition and Advice, you will remember, marks a move back to civilian, and more traditional government. In clause 1 there is a shift towards monarchy in that Cromwell himself is to choose his own successor (in the Instrument of Government, it was to be the Council, after Cromwell's death). Note also the stress on adherence to the laws of the three nations. The shift back to a two-chamber parliament is seen in clause 2. Clauses 3, 8 and 9 (which usefully indicate the chief government figures in each country) all lay great stress on the (restored) rights of parliament).

Anthology, I.25. Annesley stresses the geographical problem. It's very difficult to expose bribery, since you have to come all the way over to Westminster to do it. Those in Ireland have no control over their own taxation. He doesn't want thirty members over here, but to have Irish grievances redressed in Ireland. Then he moves on to the disproportionate taxation of Ireland compared with Scotland. The historical significance of the document is that it clearly reveals the grievances of English settlers over the position of Ireland in the Cromwellian Protectorate.

Exercise   Turn to *Anthology*, I.26. Briefly give the historical context for this document, comment on its reliability and on any other relevant points, and sum up its historical significance.

Specimen Answer and   The immediate occasion for this letter is the death of Mazarin who had
Discussion   acted as chief minister to Louis since 1653. Now Louis, nearly twenty-three, announces that he is going to run the government himself. Historically, though not necessarily in practice, the Chancellor was important as the official who kept the king's seal (Briggs mentions this, though rather obliquely). Briggs does not mention Lionne, so I cannot expect you to know, at this stage, who he was, though I hope it did occur to you that to explicate the document fully we would have to know this.

Lionne, in fact, had been a member of Louis's Council for ten years and was typical of the close-knit circle which tended to monopolize government office. A point that would be worth making here (again I don't expect you to know this) is that although Louis is assuming direct power he didn't make many changes in the ministers he used (Lionne subsequently became Secretary of Foreign Affairs). However, as I am sure you spotted, there is one important new minister: this is the document which announces the arrival of Colbert and tells us that he got there thanks to Mazarin's recommendation. The major historical significance of the document, however (and as long as you got that, you are doing pretty well) is that it marks a new stage in the political development of France after the Frondes, one approaching still closer to absolute royal control, and, on the whole, enhancing the stability of the realm. The system worked pretty well, at least in the period we are concerned with in this unit because, though intellectually limited, Louis (as Briggs tell us, p.145) had an enormous physical vitality; and an exceptionally strong will, combined with a dedication to the painstaking everyday exercise of power.

The Restoration, 1660–6

England

At the end of Chapter 7 of Coward (p.277), we read that on 16 March (1660) the Long Parliament 'declared itself dissolved'. At the beginning of Chapter 8 (p.285) we read of the Convention Parliament meeting on 25 April. In a quite astonishing gap in what is in general a most excellent textbook, Coward fails to tell us how the Convention came into being (a convention is a preliminary parliament, 'a parliament about a parliament', a parliament, in short, which, because of some interruption in due constitutional processes has not been summoned in the proper way). In fact it was the Long Parliament, before dissolving itself, which (under, of course, the surveillance of the only man with an efficient army at his heels, General Monck) issued writs for the election of a Convention, an election in which, for the first time in the Interregnum, royalists were not banned from voting. The Convention subsequently legitimized itself as a parliament. All of this strikes me as rather important: it was a parliament (with too long a shelf-life, but more representative than some) which, without a king, or even a lord protector, had summoned a convention; it was this convention, which itself decided the fundamentals of the constitutional future and then declared itself a parliament. Meantime, from his court at Breda in the Low Countries, Charles issued his dream programme (*Anthology*, I.27).

What I want you to do now is to read Coward carefully through from p.281 to p.298. Then I want you to go back and read these pages again, but this time in conjunction with the comments which follow.

Pages 281–4 form a brief overview. Coward warns us against taking 1660 as firmly and finally guaranteeing the power of parliament within a monarchical constitution. Religion remained 'a powerful, political and social force', but the effects of the English Revolution were diverse. Not everyone was sympathetic to the aspirations of militant Anglicans. In his title for Chapter 8, Coward shows clearly where he stands. 'Failure' seems a harsh word (the Commonwealth and Protectorate was a 'failure', yet had substantial achievements); without doubt the 'Settlement' was incomplete and unsatisfactory.

Page 285, paragraph 1. If 'political instability' is something narrower than 'general instability', then perhaps this is all right. But my feeling is that Coward gives an exaggerated impression of the extent of instability. However, he does, in what follows, admirably summarize the basic problems the new regime had to face, and I want to be sure that you have picked them out. But first I want you to read carefully what Coward says (top of p.286) about the Declaration of Breda. Now turn to the *Anthology*, I.27 and make sure you can find the promises identified by Coward (they actually come in the order: general pardon; religious toleration; confiscated estates). The final paragraph also has some significance. The army was paid off, as promised; but immediately disbanded, so it was no longer around to restrain extreme Anglican policies – however, probably what most appealed to most people about the Restoration was the ending of army rule. Much of your reading of the rest of Chapter 8 of Coward can be in terms of seeing how the other promises of Breda were modified or ditched.

Exercise   Bearing in mind both what you have read in Coward and the proposals made in the Declaration of Breda, what subjects would you think were most likely to be contentious enough to threaten the stability of the constitutional settlement?

Discussion   I'd suggest that there were four main areas.

1   The fundamental question of the respective powers of crown and parliament. It's worth considering whether a once-and-for-all settlement was in fact possible. Coward gives a splendid summary of the constitutional position on pp.289–90.

2   Finance and taxation. Another matter which was not finally resolved. Coward suggests some of the problems on pp.291–2.

3   Religion. Clearly still an enormous potential threat to stability, but more than that Venner's rising 'posed no real threat' (p.293) and that *had* the Act of Uniformity been assiduously enforced there might have been rebellion (p.295), but it was not and there wasn't. I see a force for stability in the way in which Protestant dissent survived (p.296).

4   Royalist lands. Sensibly dealt with (p.289).

Scotland
Here I will start with a bare summary, which you can develop by going on to read the remainder of Offprint 8.

The Resolutioners expected Presbyterianism to be established in England as well as Scotland. In fact the Scottish bishops were re-established, as was the Scottish nobility, complete with powers of appointing the local clergy. It was this reimposition of lay patronage, and the resultant exclusion of about thirty per cent of Scottish ministers, which created the clandestine Covenanting opposition and much violence, particularly in Central and South Western Scotland. There was 'half-hearted rebellion' in 1666, defeated at Rullion Green.

The Scottish parliament was restored, with the bishops again controlling the active committee, the Lords of the Articles, in the king's interest. But the bishops no longer acted as government ministers. On the whole, Mitchison suggests, the improvements in administration and tax-rising of the Cromwellian period were maintained, while, at least, Scotland was again an independent kingdom. She no longer had the handicap of English external customs duties and prohibitions, but equally lost her rights of free trade with England and English possessions.

Now, with these points in mind, read Offprint 8.

Ireland

The Restoration, while bringing back the Irish parliament, left Ireland as firmly in the grip of English power as ever. Many Catholics protested their loyalty to the crown but the determination of Protestant settlers of the 1650s to retain their lands remained an outstanding political problem. The settlement marked a further stage in the process initiated by Henry Cromwell, whereby the Protestant English were developing into a 'Protestant Ascendancy' and through the Act of Uniformity enforced the rigorous exclusion of the Catholic majority from civic life. Despite this, it has been argued that Restoration Ireland enjoyed an oasis of stability, prior to the traumas of 1688, and anticipating the stability of the eighteenth century (Foster, 1988, Chapter 6).

Social consequences

I've already mentioned the difficulties of singling out precise historical consequences; because certain developments follow a particular event, that does not mean they are necessarily consequences of that event.

In essence, there are two questions:

1   What, if any, were the changes affecting those within the political nation (in all four kingdoms and the principality)?

2   What, if any, were the changes affecting those outside the political nation?

You are not expected to give very complete answers to such questions but you should be able to offer a comment on these questions in the light of your work to date. You should also read Offprint 10, but note that this offprint refers only to England.

Exercise   Take the two questions above together (you may well have difficulty deciding who is inside and who outside the political nation) and ask them of each country in turn. Where, and among what sort of people would you expect that there might be change? Finally do you consider that there was more social change in France or in England? However scrappy your thoughts do try to write them down. But, first of all, read Offprint 10. Start by specifying the sorts of people you might expect to experience social change, then consider England since you have most on that, then do your best with the other countries.

Discussion   I specify the sorts of people as: (a) particular religious groups; (b) nobility and gentry firmly within the political nation (c) lesser gentry and bourgeoisie – those on the borders of the political nation; (d) 'ordinary people' – outside the political nation; (e) women. Then for England, I'd produce a digest of Offprint 10, organized as far as possible under these headings. I can't really improve upon his account, save that I'd add from Coward (p.264) points about lesser gentry and non-gentry becoming involved in administration during the Interregnum, and about improvement in poor law administration (p.264), touched on by Underdown. Everyone would seem agreed that there were strict limits on the gains made by women; there is the slightly ambivalent point about the growth of affective individualism. For Ireland you should concentrate on the rise of the English settlers, the 'revolution' in land-ownership, and the further degradation of the Catholic majority. For Scotland I'd specify the improvement in administration, and the overall diminution in the power of nobility, singling out the notion that 'clocks can never be put back' (Offprint 8). For both countries I'd stress the severe constraints imposed on the possibilities of social change by economic adversity. For France I'd first stress the absolutist and repressive powers of the state: from the detailed studies we've made it becomes clear how little possibility there was for change for ordinary people, the point being reinforced by the almost permanent economic adversity. We saw, too, that within the closely-knit political class there was in fact very little change. France has some very distinguished women (one thinks immediately of Madame de Sévigné), perhaps in some respects freer than their English counterparts; but of actual change there is very little evidence. Society and government were even more rigid than in England; the English civil war was a more severe crisis than the French Frondes; the English civil war and its aftermath produced more social change than did the analogous events in France, but even that was rather circumscribed.

Looking at domestic buildings

Now turn to Video 5, Domestic buildings II: Ireland and Brittany after 1630.

So far we have looked at written evidence for the return to stability in France and the British Isles in the 1650s and 1660s. But there is also evidence for this in the buildings of the period. In this exercise we shall develop the work you began in Video 4.

The exercise is devised in three parts. The first part is a study of a gentleman's house of the second half of the seventeenth century in Ireland and you should work on it in the same way that you worked on the exercises on Video 4. I will give you some information about who built the house and the circumstances in which it was put up. You should then watch Part 1 of the video and do the exercises. When you have finished, watch Part 2 for the discussion. Parts 3 and 4 of the video are rather more speculative as we know considerably less about the buildings, but is an opportunity for you to develop the techniques we have already been using.

Beaulieu House, co. Louth, Ireland

The house was probably built by Sir Henry Tichbourne (*c*.1581–1667). He was an Englishman, his father was gentleman of the privy chamber to James I. Sir Henry served as a soldier in Ireland from the 1620s and during the 1620s and 1630s received grants of land in co. Tyrone, and counties Leitrim and Donegal. He became the king's governor of Drogheda in 1641 and defended it against Catholic rebels November 1641–March 1642. He held various positions in the king's service in Ireland and was regarded with suspicion by parliament until his valiant service on behalf of the parliamentary forces against a Catholic army at Dungan's Hill in April 1647. He led a quiet existence during the Commonwealth. At the Restoration he was appointed Marshal of the Army, and in 1666 was granted an estate in co. Louth, near Drogheda, where he built a house and died in 1667. His grandson, another Sir Henry, who inherited the estate, was an ardent supporter of William III. The younger Sir Henry's daughter married William Aston, descendant of Sir Arthur Aston, defender of Drogheda against the Cromwellian forces in 1649, to whom the house passed in 1731. Sir Henry the younger certainly made some alterations to the house and may have done considerably more than that.

   The house is set on the banks of the river Boyne, near to the town of Drogheda and about 30 miles north of Dublin. Co. Louth is within the Pale, the area of Ireland settled by the Old English and within the effective jurisdiction of the government in Dublin. The land granted to Tichbourne had been confiscated from William Plunkett, member of a prominent Old English family. Drogheda was a place of some strategic importance because it commands the entrance to the river Boyne, hence the many sieges it endured during the period 1641–9.

Figure 35
An outline map of Ireland showing location of buildings featured in Video 5.

Video Exercise 1   Watch Part 1 of the video and write notes on these two questions.

1   Why has Beaulieu been built in this particular way?

2   What changes seem to have come about in Ireland between 1618 (when Monea Castle and Coppinger's Court were built, Video 4) and the later seventeenth century (when Beaulieu was built)?

Discussion   Now watch Part 2 of the video for the discussion.

Video Exercise 2   Watch Part 3 of the video, the film of the two houses in Brittany. Both houses were built by minor Breton noblemen, the first, Tronjoly, in the sixteenth century with adaptations dating from the second half of the

Figure 36
An outline map of Brittany showing location of houses featured in Video 5.

seventeenth century; the second, Kergroadès, in the first half of the seventeenth   century.

1   What do we learn about changes which have taken place in the arrangement of domestic space in the houses of lesser Breton nobles?

2   What do we learn about Breton nobles' sense of security?

Discussion   Play Part 4 of the video for the discussion.

References

Beik, W. (1985), *Absolutism and Society in Seventeenth Century France: State Power and Provincial Aristocracy in Languedoc,* Cambridge University Press, Cambridge.

Dow, F.D. (1979), *Cromwellian Scotland 1651–1660,* John Donald, Edinburgh.

Foster, R.F. (1988), *Modern Ireland, 1600–1972,* Allen Lane and The Penguin Press, London.

Golden, R. M. (1981), *The Godly Rebellion: Parisian Curés and the Religious Fronde, 1652–1662,* University of North Carolina Press, Chapel Hill.

Underdown, D. (1987), *Revel, Riot and Rebellion: Popular Politics and Culture in England 1603–1660,* Clarendon Press, Oxford.

Index

absolutism 11
  France as absolutist state 1, 6
agriculture, in England 70, 71, 107
Alexander, William, first Earl of Stirling 55–7, 61
ambassadors, reception of 39–40
Anne of Austria, Queen of France 43, 52, 53, 54, 57
  and the Frondes 89, 90
  regency 101, 106
Anne of Denmark, Queen of England 45
Anne, Queen 10
army, the, and the Protectorate 130, 131
assemblies 17–18
Aston, Sir Arthur 155

Bate, John 22
Battifol, L. 40, 41, 52, 53
Beaulieu House, Ireland 155
Bercé, Yves-Marie 7
Bergin, Joseph 111
Bishop's Wars (1639–40) 62, 67, 73, 75, 101, 121
Bonney, R. 14, 19, 91, 92, 103, 110
Booth's Rebellion (1659) 142–3, 149
Bordeaux
  economic problems and riots in 59, 77–9
  Ormée movement 90–1, 91–2
Bossuet, Jacques Bénigne 114
Boulonnais revolt (1662) 138, 145–7
Breda, Declaration of 151, 152
Brittany, buildings in 154, 155–6
Broussel, Pierre 90, 91
Buckingham, George Villiers, Duke of 12, 25, 41, 42, 58
  and the Duchess of Chevreuse 52, 53
  portrait 41
buildings
  in Brittany 154, 155–6
  in Ireland 117–19, 154–5
  of monarchs 45
  in rural areas 30–3

Cadillac, Château de 49, 51
Catholicism see Roman Catholicism
Chalais affair 53
Chambre Saint Louis, and the Fronde of the *parlements* 90
Charles I, king of Scotland and England 10, 16, 44
  and the civil wars 61–3, 69, 93, 112, 114, 121
  collections 45–6
  and divine right 12
  and the Duchess of Chevreuse 52, 53

  and the Earl of Stirling 55, 56, 57
  foreign policy 110
  and the government of Scotland 61–2, 104, 105
  and the 'Incident' 74, 75
  and literature 46
  and manufacturing industries 107
  masques and court ballets 47
  and the nobility 48
  portrait 37, 44–5
  problems of implementing policies 60
  religious policies 58, 60, 61
  responsibility for the civil war 61–3
  and revisionist historians 112
  and the royal court 37, 38, 39–40, 43, 57
  and royal favourites 42, 58
  as ruler of a multiple kingdom 121, 122, 123
  and the Scottish Revolution 73–5
  and taxes 58–9, 108
Charles II, king of Scotland and England 114, 142, 151
Chevreuse, Claude de Lorraine, Duke of 41, 52, 53, 54
Chevreuse, Marie-Aimée, Duchess of 52–4, 57, 60
Church of England 14, 23, 68
Church of Ireland 14–15
Church of Scotland 15, 68
church, the
  and taxes 23
  see also religion
civil wars 99–100
  causes of 69–73
  constitutional consequences 149–50
  course of 80–1
  economic factors 70–1, 80
  and economic infrastructure 107–8
  particular and local explanations of 114–16
  and politics 72–3, 80, 109–10
  and religion 73, 80, 93, 94
  social factors 71–2, 80
  see also English civil war; Irish rebellion; Scottish Revolution
Clarendon, Edward Hyde, 1st Earl of, *History of the Rebellion and Civil Wars in England* 100
Clubmen movement 81
Colbert, Jean-Baptiste 137, 138, 145, 151
Collège de Quatre Nations 13
Committee of Safety 131
comparative history 6–9
Condé, Louis, Prince de 50, 90, 92, 114, 140
constitutional consequences
  Frondes 149, 150–1, 151